World Hospitality Cookbook

World Hospitality Cookbook

Edited by
Erma I. Sider
and
Dan & Betty Harman

Evangel
Publishing House
Nappanee, Indiana 46550

Evangel Publishing House
P.O. Box 189
2000 Evangel Way
Nappanee, Indiana 46550-0189

Toll-Free Order Line: (800) 253-9315
Internet Website: www.evangelpublishing.com

Publisher's Cataloging-in-Publication
(Provided by Quality Books, Inc.)

World hospitality cookbook / edited by Erma I. Sider and Dan & Betty Harman.

    p. cm.
    Includes index.
    LCCN 2002107253
    ISBN 1-928915-34-5

    1. Cookery, International. 2. Menus. 3. Food habits. I. Sider, Erma I. II. Harman, Dan. III. Harman, Betty, 1933–

TX725.A1W675 2003   641.59
                        QBI03-200623

Printed in the United States of America

03 04 05 06 07 / 5 4 3 2 1

TABLE OF CONTENTS

Publisher's Preface

We should be closer to one another than ever before. High-speed communication and jet travel enable us to go from one continent to another in a few hours' time and to conduct a conversation with anyone in the world in "real time."

Even so, other forces are pushing us apart. Political unrest, competition for scarce resources, and lingering suspicion about old enemies cause us to withdraw into tribal or national enclaves, where we fear we may be maimed by foreign terrorists or plundered by our own neighbors. One curious statistic helps to explain why we live in such a climate of apprehension:

> The vast majority of people—98 percent—stay home and never move beyond the boundaries of their own countries. Of these, many have significant exposure to other cultures because people have moved to their countries and communities, but in some parts of the world, there is relatively little knowledge of or exposure to other peoples, cultures and customs. Even where there is the opportunity, other priorities can keep us ignorant. The world is still a big place.[1]

Perhaps we shall always have a certain degree of ignorance about the other people of our world, but we do not need to live in fear of them. We have no reason to harbor hostility toward those who dress differently, speak a different language, or observe different customs of daily life.

This is especially true of Christians. Jesus Christ calls His followers to be world citizens. He urges us to "go into all the world and preach the good news to all creation" (Mark 16:15). We are not devoted to one culture, one political ideology, or one set of social customs. Instead we are devoted to the One who created all the peoples of the earth, and we have the privilege of inviting them to meet Him.

The *World Hospitality Cookbook* was compiled by Christian missionaries who share what they have learned of the food and hospitality customs of other countries. They hope it will help to draw people closer together, because the simple act of sharing one another's food can lead us to a deeper appreciation of one another. One of the compilers, writes:

Because we have experienced hospitality in many parts of the world, we know exactly what the apostle Paul was talking about when he described the generosity of the Macedonians: "Out of the most severe trial, their overflowing joy and their extreme poverty welled up in rich generosity. . . . They gave as much as they were able, and even beyond their ability" (2 Cor. 8:2–3).[2]

May you experience this kind of hospitality as you come to know more people from other cultures. May you extend this hospitality toward others as a result of reading this book.

Proceeds from the sale of this book support the work of Brethren in Christ World Missions.

---

[1]Erma I. Sider, ed., *Celebration of Hospitality* (Nappanee, Indiana: Evangel, 1997), 4.

[2]*Celebration of Hospitality*, 5.

Appetizers, Beverages, Breads, and Soups

Hospitality in Argentina

Argentineans are justifiably proud of their excellent and inexpensive steaks. Indeed, in many homes a steak is prepared for guests in addition to whatever the main course of the meal might be. All airline flights originating in South America serve Argentinean meats, exclusively. Plain broiled steaks are common, but creative chefs pride themselves on delicious sauces for basting or marinating of their beef. In modern Argentina, fruits and vegetables often are cooked with the meats, providing all-in-one meals.

In general, Argentineans eat little or no breakfast. When they do, it may consist only of coffee and toast with butter and jam. But their mid-morning snack includes coffee and a *tostado*—a sandwich comprised of thin-toasted bread, ham, and cheese—and a glass of freshly squeezed orange juice.

In Buenos Aires, *the* city of Argentina, the business day routinely is broken many times for what Americans would call a coffee break. The most common snack at these times is maté con facturas, maté with sweet pastries. In fact, as one veteran traveler in South America put it, "If you want to impress your hostess when you are invited to an Argentine home, stop by a bakery on the way and pick up some maté con facturas. You will be welcomed with open arms."

The Argentina cowboy-gauchos' famous heavy diet of steak might be the envy of many teenagers around the world. With so many cattle and so many months away from home, the gauchos subsist almost entirely on beef and maté. The gauchos kill a head of beef, roast the entire animal in its own hide (a process called asado con cuero), then eat the beef and drink the maté till it's gone. (For a more sophisticated version of this meal, see our recipe for Sautéed Steak and Potatoes.)

Argentineans are fond of nutritious yellow-fleshed winter squash. They are creative in using it for soups, fritters, and a sort of baked squash pudding that is like a squash pie without the crust. Perhaps the most appealing squash dish is carbonada criolla, an elaborate beef stew that is baked inside a squash, using the strong-shelled vegetable as a casserole dish that can be eaten.

Spiced Tea
Nepal

Chia
(chee-ah)

Serves 10

Wonderful on a cold, chilly, and damp day to escape the gloom!

Bring to a full boil:
>   **10 c. water**

Add:
>   **5 tea bags or 5 t. loose tea**
>   **2 c. milk, heated**
>   **8 whole cloves**
>   **1 t. ground cardamom**
>   **2 cinnamon sticks**

Steep 5 to 10 minutes. Serve hot.

—Esther Lenhert
Kathmandu, Nepal

Fruit Drink
Venezuela

Batidos
(bah-TEE-dohs)

These drinks are served in restaurants, streetside coffee shops, and at home. They are very refreshing on a hot day.

Combine in a blender:
>   **½–¾ c. fresh fruit**
>   **2 c. water**
>   **2–4 T. sugar, as desired**
>   **5–6 ice cubes, one at a time**

Serve immediately.

Variations:
Use chunks of frozen fruit and omit ice cubes.
Use milk instead of water.
Use any fruit or combination of fruit:
Watermelon, strawberries, cantaloupe, papaya, pineapple, mango.
For an exotic and exquisite flavor, try orange passion fruit and granadine syrup.

—Martha Giles
Caracas, Venezuela

Herbal Tea
Argentina

Maté
(MAH-tay)

Serves 4–6

Maté (Ilex Paraguensis) is a large shrub whose leaves are dried and brewed as tea. Many people drink maté tea as a tonic, so the leaves are usually available at health-food stores. Look for the generic name, "yerba maté."

Combine in a teapot:
> **3 T. maté**
> **3 t. sugar**
> **4 c. hot water**

Steep for 5–7 minutes, strain if desired. Serve with a dash of lemon juice.

Individual Servings:
Hot *(Maté Cocida)*: For each cup, combine **2 T. maté** and **1 t. sugar** in a teapot. Add **1 c. hot, but not boiling, water**. Let steep 5 minutes.

Iced *(Maté Tetre)*: Mix the same portions of maté, sugar, and hot water. Cover and let stand for 20 minutes. Strain and add lemon juice. Chill, then serve over ice in tall glasses.

Yogurt Freshener
Nepal

Lassi
(LAH-see)

Mix all ingredients:
> **1 qt. milk**
> **1 qt. yogurt**
> **½–¾ c. sugar**
> **4 t. vanilla**
> **6–8 dry mint leaves**

Let stand in refrigerator at least 5 hours.

—Esther Lenhert
Kathmandu, Nepal

Pumpkin Punch
Colombia

Jugo de Auyama
(WHO-go day
Ow-YAH-mah)

Serves 8

Combine in blender:
   2 c. pumpkin, cooked
   3-oz. package strawberry Jell-O®
   2+ c. milk
Add sugar as desired. Serve very cold.

Options:
Other flavors of Jell-O® can be used, and cranberry is especially satisfying.

—*Gloria Hernández de Silva*
Bogota, Colombia

The highest point in Africa is Mt. Kiliminjaro in Tanzania. Photo © Corbis.

13

Lemon Barley Water
England

Wash:

2 T. pearl barley

Put in a large pan with:

4 cups water

Bring to a boil, then add:

Grated rind of 2 lemons

Cover and allow to cool. Squeeze the lemons and add the juice to the above mixture. Strain the mixture through a sieve. Sweeten to taste.

—*Judy Smith*
London, England

Tea Scones
Zimbabwe

Makes 16

When the missionaries spent a day shopping in Bulawayo, Zimbabwe, the tradition was to meet at Haddon and Sly Tea Lounge about mid-morning for tea and toasted scones.

Measure into bowl:

2 c. flour
3 T. sugar
3 t. baking powder
¼ t. salt

Chop with pastry blender, adding:

⅓ c. margarine

Combine the following ingredients and pour into above:

1 egg, beaten
½ c. milk

Stir quickly and lightly until no flour shows. Add more milk if needed to make a soft dough. Turn the dough out on a floured surface and knead gently about one minute. Roll out about one-half inch thick; cut into 2" rounds. Place on ungreased baking sheet; bake at 425° for 12 minutes. Serve warm.

—*Erma Hoover*
Zimbabwe

Fastnachts
United States/ Pennsylvania Dutch

Fastnacht
(Fasht-NAHKT)

Makes 4 dozen

Fastnacht Day is the day before Lent begins. The custom began as a way to use up all the fat before the beginning of Lent. Our extended family gathers at our home to make fastnachts.

Dissolve in ¼ **c. warm water:**
> **2 oz. cake yeast**

Add and mix:
> **4 c. warm water**
> **1 c. sugar**
> **⅔ c. shortening, melted**
> **2 T. salt**

Add gradually and knead:
> **3½ lb. flour**

Place dough in a bowl, cover with cloth and allow to rise 1 hour. Remove dough from bowl and roll out 2" thick (use desired size biscuit cutter) and cut fastnachts. Let rise again for 1 hour. Then fry in deep fat until each side is lightly browned.

—*Janie Hess*
Conestoga, PA

The Lord's Table and Our Tables

What does [the Lord's Table] imply about our tables? First, hospitable meals are generous. At the table, God gives His very best, so we too should strive to offer the best meals we can. It's not a matter of showing off culinary skills, but of sharing from the abundance God has given....

Second, hospitable meals are nutritious and filling. Therefore, we should seek to provide a healthy diet, not just platefuls of empty calories....

Finally, the Lord's table offers celebration. Like the wine that makes the heart glad, our meals should offer pleasing tastes. We should strive to set a table where guests can savor the richness of God's provision, relax, and enjoy. Our good meals can serve as a conduit for guests to "taste and see that the Lord is good."

—Laurel Webster Garver,
"Gaining a Christian Vision for Hospitality,"
Meresheth Magazine, June 3, 2003

Danish Doughnuts
Denmark

Aebleskiver
(EYE-buhl-ski-VERR)

Makes 15–20

Sift together:
> 4½ c. plain flour
> 2 t. baking powder

Then add:
> 1 t. ground cardamom or grated lemon rind

Stir in:
> ½ c. milk
> 2 egg yolks
> 2 T. melted butter

Add:
> ¼ t. salt
> 1 T. granulated sugar

Stir to a fairly thick, smooth batter. Beat until stiff:
> 2 egg whites

Fold them lightly into the batter. Pour a little melted butter into each cup of a heated doughnut pan and then fill the cup two-thirds full of batter. Cook over medium heat for about 3 minutes, until doughnuts are set underneath. Turn them over and finish cooking on the other side for 2–3 minutes, until they are golden all over. Serve hot with powdered sugar sprinkled over both sides of doughnuts.

Variation:
Place a teaspoon of jam or a thin slice of raw apple in the center of each doughnut before turning it over.

The Ultimate Act

The ultimate act of hospitality was when Jesus Christ died for sinners to make everyone who believes a member of the household of God. We are no longer strangers and sojourners. We have come home to God. Everybody who trusts in Jesus finds a home in God.

—John Piper

Russian Pancakes
Russia

Blini
(BLEE-nee)

Serves 6–8

Scald **2 c. milk,** then cool to lukewarm. Pour into a deep bowl and crumble into it ½ **cake yeast.** Stir until smooth. Stir in:

2 t. sugar
1½ c. flour

Cover bowl with cloth and set in a warm place for 1½ hrs. for the mixture ("sponge") to rise. In a separate bowl, combine:

3 egg yolks
5 T. butter, softened
1 t. salt
1½ c. flour

Then mix this with the sponge. Beat well and put aside to rise again for another 1½ hrs. Stiffly whip:

3 egg whites

Stir these into the batter with a fork. Let mixture stand 10 minutes before you begin making pancakes.

English Scones
Canada

Makes 12

Stir together in a large bowl:

2¼ c. flour
2 T. granulated sugar
2½ t. baking powder
½ t. baking soda
½ t. salt

Using a pastry blender, cut in the following until mixture resembles coarse crumbs:

½ c. cold butter, cubed

Stir in:

½ c. currants

Add the following all at once, stirring with fork to make soft, sticky dough:

1 c. buttermilk

With lightly-floured hands, press dough into a ball. On lightly-floured surface, knead gently 10 times. Pat dough into ¾" high round. Cut into 2½" rounds. Place on ungreased baking sheet. Bake at 425° for 12–15 minutes. Serve with jam and/or whipped, unsweetened cream.

—Laureen Cinder
Elizabethtown, PA

Siberian Rolls
Russia

Makes 3–4 dozen rolls

Dissolve **3 T. yeast** in **¼ c. lukewarm water** and allow it to become foamy and thick. Mix in:

> **3 c. whole wheat flour**
> **1½ c. milk**

Allow this batter to rise. Then add:

> **6 egg yolks, beaten**
> **1 c. butter, softened**
> **¾ c. sugar**
> **2 t. salt**
> **3 c. whole wheat flour**

Knead dough until smooth. Let rise 1½–2 hrs. Shape into round, flat rolls. Place 1" apart on a greased baking sheet and let rise until almost double in size. In a separate bowl, beat:

> **2 T. sour cream**
> **1 T. butter, softened**
> **2 T. white flour**

Brush this glaze onto the rolls. Bake in oven at 375° for 20–30 minutes.

Brazilian Cheese Rolls
Brazil

Pai de Queijo
(PAY duh QWEE-yo)

Makes 12 rolls

These cheese rolls are one of the most popular appetizers in Brazil. The tapioca flour produces a light consistency that Brazilians love.

Preheat oven to 450° F. Sift **1⅔ c. tapioca flour**. In saucepan, combine:

> **4 T. sunflower oil**
> **generous pinch of sea salt**
> **6 T. water**

Bring to boil. Slowly pour this mixture onto the flour, stirring it to a stiff dough with wooden spoon. When dough has cooled slightly, stir in:

> **1 egg, beaten**
> **6 T. plain yogurt**
> **½ c. freshly grated cheese, preferably Parmesan**

Grease hands with a piece of paper towel dampened with vegetable oil, then form dough into twelve balls. Arrange on nonstick baking sheet. Put into oven and immediately lower temperature to 350°. Bake 25–30 minutes. Test for doneness with skewer. (If it comes out clean, they're done.) Cool on wire rack.

My Favorite Bread
Québec

Mon Pain Preferé
(mohn PAN preh-fair-AY)

Makes 4 loaves

Dissolve **2 T. (2 pkgs.) dry yeast in ½ c. warm water.** Add:

> **1 t. sugar**
> **¼ t. ginger**

Set this yeast mixture aside. Mix together in a large bowl:

> **⅓ c. sugar**
> **¾ c. dry milk powder**
> **2½ c. warm water**
> **4 c. all-purpose flour (or 2 c. whole wheat, 2 c. white)**

Add yeast mixture. Mix to a smooth batter; beat well. Allow it to rise until light and bubbly (about 15 minutes.) Stir down and add:

> **3 c. warm water**
> **5 t. salt**
> **½ c. shortening or lard**
> **8 c. white bread flour (approx.)**

Knead 5 minutes, using additional flour if necessary. Place in greased bowl, turn, and let rise until double (approx. 1 hour). Punch down. Divide dough into 4 parts and shape into loaves. Place in greased 9"x5" bread pans. Cover and let rise 45 minutes. Bake at 350° for 25 minutes, then at 325° for 20 minutes.

> —*Sylvie St-Hilaire*
> *St. Romuald, Québec*

Black Bread
Russia

Makes 2 medium loaves

Dissolve **1 pkg. yeast** in ¼ **c. lukewarm water**. Allow to become foamy. Then pour into bowl and add:

> **1 T. white sugar**
> **1½ c. bread flour**
> **1½ c. medium rye flour**
> **¼ c. whole wheat flour**
> **½ c. unprocessed bran flakes**
> **1 T. caraway seeds**
> **1 t. salt**
> **1 t. instant coffee**
> **¼ t. fennel seeds**

Combine the following in a saucepan over low heat until chocolate and butter melt, stirring frequently:

> **1 c. + 2 T. water**
> **2 T. vinegar**
> **2 T. molasses**
> **2 T. butter**
> **½ oz. unsweetened chocolate**

Add to flour mixture and mix until it becomes a stiff dough, then allow to rise 1½–2 hrs. Knead and let rise again, then bake in two loaf pans at 350° for 25–35 minutes.

Kneeldown Bread
New Mexico/ Navajo Indian

Makes 3 small loaves

This is called kneeldown bread because the cook has to kneel down in order to grind the corn.

Scrape the kernels from **6 ears of fresh corn** on the cob. Grind it on a *metate* (a flat stone) or use a food processor to finely chop the corn. Don't completely grind it to a smooth paste, as it should still be slightly chunky. Shape the ground corn into small loaves about 4"x12" in size. Wrap them in several layers of fresh green corn husks. Bake either in hot campfire ashes or in an oven at medium-low temperature for at least one hour. Remove from husks and eat at once.

> —*Karen Redfearn*
> *New Mexico*

Fry Bread
New Mexico /
Navajo Indian

Serves 12

Mix together in a large bowl:
> **4 c. flour**
> **1 T. baking powder**
> **1 t. salt**
> **2 T. powdered milk**

Add gradually, mixing with a fork:
> **1½ c. warm water (more or less)**

Make a soft dough. Cover. Let rest 10–20 minutes. In an electric fry pan, heat 1" vegetable oil to 400°–425°. Divide dough into 12 pieces. Flatten and pull a piece of dough into a flat round (about 6" in diameter). Fry in hot oil, turning once until brown on both sides, about 12 minutes on each side. Serve at once.

Tortilla variation:
To the above dry ingredients add:
> **3 T. shortening**

Cook in a dry pan about 20 seconds on each side.

Taco shell variation (Serves 9):
> **3 c. flour**
> **2½ t. baking powder**
> **2 t. salt**
> **2 T. powdered milk**
> **1 c. + 1 T. water**

Dough can be made 6 hours ahead and fried when ready to eat. Flatten and fry in hot vegetable oil.

> —*Millie Imboden*
> *Mechanicsburg, PA*

Festive Ham Bread
Venezuela

Pan de Jamón
(Pahn day hah-MOHN)

This favorite Venezuelan Christmas treat is also served at many special church functions.

Make your favorite white bread recipe for 2 loaves. Let rise, punch down, and divide into halves. (Or defrost 2 loaves of frozen bread dough.) Roll each into a rectangle approximately 3" thick. Spread lightly with bacon grease, margarine, or mustard, if desired. Layer on top each rectangle:

> ¼ lb. cooked ham, sliced or diced
> ⅓ c. bacon, fried and crumbled
> ⅓–½ c. stuffed olives, sliced
> ⅓–½ c. raisins

Roll up dough as for jelly roll, turning ends under, and place on greased cookie sheet, seam side down. Do not let rise, but bake immediately at 350° for 30–35 minutes. Vary the amounts and kinds of ingredients according to taste.

When bread has cooled slightly, cut into 1" slices. It can be sliced thinner or thicker, depending upon the number of people to serve. Serve hot or cold.

—*Martha Giles, Niagara Falls, ON,
and Sherry Holland, Caracas,
Venezuela*

Don't Worry—They Won't Eat Much!

"The tummy of a traveller is no larger than the horn of a goat." This Zimbabwean phrase means that travellers should not be denied any refreshment if they turn up unexpectedly. The rationale: They would eat so little that it would fit into the horn of a goat.

—Doris Dube
Bulawayo, Zimbabwe

Village women cook rice together in Zimbabwe.

Fresh Cornbread
Zimbabwe

Serves 6

My mother used to bake fresh cornbread in a three-legged pot. She would put sand in the pot and put charcoal on the lid and under the pot. When the pot was hot, she would put the mixture in a metal bowl and bake it inside the black pot. This was a delicacy for her children who returned home for school vacation from mission centers at Matapo, Wanezi, and Mtshabezi.

Combine these ingredients, mixing thoroughly:

2 c. corn, fresh or frozen
1 t. salt
½ c. flour
1 t. sugar
1½ t. baking powder
3 T. vegetable oil
½ c. milk

Pour into a greased baking dish. Bake at 350° for 45–60 minutes or until golden brown. May be served with a meal or with syrup for tea.

—*Martha Sibanda*
Diana's Pool, Zimbabwe

Wheat (White) Bread
Germany

Weizenbrot
(wie-zen-BROT)

Makes 1 loaf

Combine in a large mixing bowl, then beat until smooth and elastic:

> **5½ c. sifted unbleached all-purpose flour**
> **1 pkg. active dry yeast**
> **2 t. salt**
> **2 c. warm water (105–115° F.)**

This is hard work, so use a heavy-duty food processor or mixer with dough hook if you can, mixing for one minute exactly, then let the dough rest and cool for 5 minutes. (With processor or mixer, be careful not to overheat dough by mixing too long; this kills the yeast.)

Beat dough for 30 seconds by machine again, and let it rest for 5 minutes. Repeat the beating and resting process four more times. Scoop the dough into a well-buttered, warm, large bowl. With well-buttered hands, pat the surface of the dough so it's nicely buttered too. Cover with a clean, dry cloth and set to rise in a warm, dry spot, away from drafts until doubled in bulk. This takes about an hour.

Toward end of rising, spread a pastry cloth on the counter and sprinkle with **4 c. of flour**. Punch dough down, place on floured cloth, and sift another **4 c. flour** on top. Gently and carefully knead in the flour. At first dough will be very sticky, but keep adding flour, 4 c. at a time, and kneading it in until dough is smooth and elastic.

Once the dough is of a good, manageable consistency, knead hard for 10 minutes. This extra kneading gives bread its firm, chewy texture. Shape dough into oval loaf 9–10" long and 4–5" wide and place on a lightly floured baking sheet. Cover with cloth and let rise in a warm, dry, draft-free spot for 30 minutes.

Preheat oven to 400° F. Bake bread one hour until nicely tan and hollow-sounding when thumped. Remove from oven, transfer to wire rack, and cool at room temperature. Cut crosswise, slightly on the bias, about 2" thick, using a sharp, serrated knife.

Black Forest Hazelnut Bread
Germany

Schwarzwalder Haselnussbrot
(SHWARTZ-wall-dur hoss-EL-nus-BROT)

Makes 1 loaf

Preheat oven to 375° F. Butter a 9"x5"x3" loaf pan and set aside. Combine in large mixing bowl:

> **2 c. sifted all-purpose flour**
> **½ cup unsifted whole wheat flour**
> **⅓ c. firmly packed light brown sugar**
> **1 t. baking soda**
> **½ t. salt**
> **1½ t. baking powder**
> **½ t. freshly grated nutmeg**
> **¼ t. freshly ground black pepper**

Press out all lumps of sugar with your hands. Add:

> **1¼ c. finely ground, toasted, blanched hazelnuts (*see note below)**

Toss to mix, then make a well in the middle of the dry ingredients. In a 1-qt. measuring cup, whisk until creamy:

> **3 c. corn oil**
> **1 c. sour milk or buttermilk**
> **1 extra-large egg, lightly beaten**

Pour this mixture all at once into the well in the dry ingredients and stir just enough to mix; the batter should be lumpy. (Don't over-mix or bread will be tough.)

Spoon the batter into the prepared loaf pan, smoothing the top and spreading well into the corners. Bake uncovered about 45 minutes or until the bread is richly browned and sounds hollow when thumped. Cool the bread in the upright pan on a wire rack for 15 minutes. Loosen carefully around the edges with a small spatula and turn the bread out on the rack. Turn right-side-up and cool several hours before slicing.

(*Note*: To blanch and toast hazelnuts, spread the nuts in a baking pan and set in a preheated 350° oven for 30–35 minutes. Cool 10 minutes, bundle in a clean tea towel, and rub briskly to remove the skins. Don't worry about any stubborn bits clinging to the nuts; these will add color to the bread. Finely grind the hazelnuts in a food processor fitted with the metal chopping blade. One 15-second churning, a quick scraping down of the sides of the work bowl, then several fast pulses should do the job nicely; but proceed carefully and don't churn the nuts to paste.)

Coconut Bread
Brazil

Pao de Coco
(Pay-oh day CO-co)

Makes 2 loaves

Preheat oven to 350° F. Mix together in a large bowl:

2½ c. all-purpose flour
1 T. baking powder
1 t. salt
3 c. freshly grated coconut

In a 1-qt. measuring cup, whisk together until evenly mixed:

6 T. evaporated milk
1 egg, beaten
2 c. (one stick) + 1 T. butter, melted
2 c. + 2 T. sugar
2 t. vanilla extract

Scoop out a well in the center of flour-and-coconut mixture and pour in the liquid ingredients. Beat together to make a soft batter.

Divide batter between 2 buttered 9"x5" loaf pans, filling them halfway. Bake for 50 minutes to an hour. Test in center with metal skewer; bread is done when skewer comes out clean. Remove from oven and let cool in pans for 10 minutes. Unmold onto wire rack to finish cooling.

French Bread
France

Makes 1 loaf

Dissolve **2 pkgs. (5 t.) active dry yeast** in **1¾ c. warm water** (105°–115° F.). Then combine in a mixing bowl:

2 t. sugar
2 t. salt
5 c. bread flour

Add yeast liquid along with **1 T. vegetable oil**. When thoroughly mixed, add **3½–4 cups bread flour**, reserving a small portion for kneading. Knead and add small amounts of flour as needed for about 6–8 minutes, until dough is smooth and elastic.

Let rise until double. Punch down and form into loaf of desired size. Place on cookie sheet. When loaves are again double, bake at 400° F. until golden brown, about 20–25 minutes.

—William Trimble

Caraway and Fennel Seed Bread
Scandinavia

This recipe is a variation of traditional Swedish limpa *bread.*

Makes 1 loaf

Heat in a saucepan until the sugar has dissolved and the mixture is lukewarm:

> **1¼ cups water**
> **1 t. caraway seeds**
> **1 T. fennel seeds**
> **grated rind of 1 orange**

Lower heat and crumble **½ T. compressed yeast** into liquid and stir until dissolved. Pour into large bowl and add:

> **3 c. bread flour or all-purpose flour**
> **1 T. olive oil**
> **4 c. (firmly packed) brown sugar**

Stir ingredients well. Cover and leave in warm place for 30 minutes until bubbling. Then stir into the fermenting mixture:

> **2 c. rye flour**
> **1 t. salt**

Turn the dough out onto a work surface and knead thoroughly, adding a little extra white flour if necessary to make a soft but manageable dough. Place in clean bowl, cover, and leave in warm place for about 1 hour or until doubled in bulk.

Punch the dough down and knead, then shape and place in an oiled 8½"x4½"x2½" bread pan. Cover and leave to proof again for 45 minutes or until the dough has risen to top of pan. Bake bread in preheated 350° F. oven for 45 minutes. Turn loaf out on a wire rack and allow to cool before serving.

Respect Your Guest

Whether a child or an old man or a youth come to thy house, he is to be treated with respect, for of all men thy guest is thy superior.

—Sanskrit proverb

Country Bread
France

Makes 1 large loaf

Crumble **1 oz. compressed yeast** into **1½ c. lukewarm water** and leave for 3–4 minutes, then stir to completely dissolve the yeast. Mix together in a large bowl:

¾ c. whole wheat flour
4 c. all-purpose flour or bread flour
1 T. salt

Make a well in the center of these dry ingredients, then add the yeast liquid and mix to a firm dough.

Turn out onto a floured surface and knead for about 10 minutes until dough is smooth and elastic in texture. Return dough to bowl, cover, and leave in a warm place for about an hour or until doubled in bulk.

Punch dough down and reshape it, then return it to the bowl, cover, and leave it for another 30 minutes in a warm place. Lightly flour a baking sheet. Knead dough again and shape it into a round loaf. Place on baking sheet, surround it with a clean, folded cloth so that it holds its shape and rises upward. Cover and proof again for 45 minutes or until doubled in bulk.

Score bread deeply three times, then bake in preheated 475° F. oven 30–35 minutes. Cool on wire rack.

Native American children bake bannock on sticks over an open fire.

Pesto Sticks
Italy

Makes 12–18 bread sticks

Crumble ½ **oz. compressed yeast** in ½ **c. lukewarm water** and leave 3–4 minutes, then stir to completely dissolve yeast. Mix in a bowl:

2 c. bread flour or all-purpose flour
large pinch of salt

Add the yeast liquid with **2 T. olive oil**. Mix together, then turn onto a floured surface and knead into a smooth, pliable dough.

Return to bowl, cover, and leave for 1 hour in a warm place until doubled in bulk. Punch the dough down gently, then roll it out into an oblong layer about 7"x10". Spread with **2 T. pesto sauce**, leaving a narrow margin all around the edge. Roll the dough up like a jelly roll, starting from one of the long sides. Place it on a floured baking tray, seam side down. Cover and let rise another 20 minutes.

Brush olive oil over the loaf, slash the surface with a sharp blade, and bake in a preheated 400° F. oven for 30 minutes or until the loaf is golden brown. Cool on wire rack, then cut into sticks and serve.

Bannock
Northern Canada /Cree and Dene Indians

Serves 8–10

Bannock dough can be wrapped around the end of a stick (called a "grease stick") and baked over hot coals. It is traditional for the Native People to sit around their campfire at the end of the day, bake bannock on a stick, tell stories, and drink tea.

Mix together like biscuit dough:

2½ c. flour
2 t. baking powder
1 t. salt
½ c. lard

Add:

approx. 1 c. water

Stir until dough clings together, then knead on floured surface. Pat dough to 1" thickness and prick with a fork. Bake on cookie sheet at 350°–375° until well done. The Native People spread lard, margarine, or jam on bannock when it is eaten.

—*Jennie Rensberry*
LaLoche, Saskatchewan
Marlene Comfort
LaRonge, Saskatchewan
Greg Charles
Saskatchewan

Blueberry Muffins
Northern Canada / Cree Indians

Makes 12 muffins

These are a favorite food in the fall when blueberries are fresh.

Combine:

2 c. all-purpose flour, sifted
3 t. baking powder
3 t. sugar
¼ t. salt
¾ t. cinnamon

Combine and add to dry ingredients, stirring only enough to moisten:

¾ c. milk
1 egg
½ c. butter, melted

Fold in:

1 c. blueberries

Fill each muffin tin ⅔ full. Bake for 25 minutes at 400°.

—Ricky Sanderson
Saskatchewan

Cornbread Dressing
Southern United States

Serves 12

Sauté in a skillet:

1 c. celery, chopped
¼ c. onions, chopped
¾ c. butter or margarine

Pour this celery mixture into a large bowl and add:

5 c. biscuits or dry bread cubes, crumbled
5 c. cornbread, crumbled
1 t. poultry seasoning
½ t. pepper
4 c. (2 14.2-oz. cans) chicken broth

Blend well and spread in a greased 9"x13" pan. Bake at 350° for 1 hour or until lightly browned. Serve with chicken or turkey.

—Jodie Martin
Smithville, TN

Egg-Lemon Soup
Greece

Serves 6–8

Greek families do not all eat at the same time. Because of busy work schedules, soups are prepared in the morning before the wife goes to the field. When a family member comes home, the soopa is heated.

Prepare **7–8 c. soup stock** by boiling **1 whole chicken** or **2 chicken breasts** in sufficient water. Salt to taste. Debone the chicken (if bones remain), then add:
> **½–1 c. uncooked rice**

Mix in small bowl with a small amount of cooled stock:
> **1 T. cornstarch**
> **2 eggs, beaten**

Slowly stir into the rice and chicken mixture. Be careful it does not become stringy. Remove from heat. Add:
> **1 T. butter or margarine**

Slowly stir in:
> **juice of ½ lemon**

Season with:
> **salt and pepper to taste**

If desired, when serving, top with:
> **1 t. parsley, chopped**

—Beulah Heisey
Mechanicsburg, PA

Egg and Lemon Soup
England

Serves 4

Put in a saucepan and bring to a boil:
> **6 c. chicken stock**

Add and simmer for 15 minutes or until tender:
> **1 c. rice**

Mix in a separate bowl:
> **4 eggs, well beaten**
> **juice of 2 lemons**

Stir in a few spoonfuls of chicken stock. Stir this mixture into the remaining stock. Cook gently for 3 minutes. Season to taste with salt and pepper.

—June Simmonds
London, England

Peanut Soup
Zambia

Serves 6

Soak overnight:

2 c. raw peanuts

Drain off water. Add **½ t. vegetable oil** to nuts and water to cover. Simmer 1½ hours or in pressure cooker for 20 minutes. Sauté and set aside:

3 large tomatoes, cut in wedges
1 green pepper, diced
½ large onion, diced

Brown:

¾ lb. hamburger
remainder of onion, diced

Combine peanuts, tomato mixture, and meat. Add and simmer 20–30 minutes:

1½ c. water
2 c. tomato juice
2 cubes beef bouillon
1½ t. chili powder
½ t. chili seasoning mix (optional)
¼ t. garlic powder
2 T. ketchup
1½ t. salt
dash of oregano
3 T. sugar

The secret of this soup is to keep on tasting it as you add seasonings until you reach the desired flavor. The amount of seasonings can be altered to suit individual tastes. Serve any time soup is appropriate. It goes nicely with bran muffins and also with rice or stiff cornmeal porridge *(nshima)*.

—*Phyllis A. Engle*
Livingstone, Zambia

Pumpkin Soup
Venezuela

Crema de Auyama
(CREE-mah day ow-YAH-mah)

Serves 4–6

Heat **1 T. margarine or oil** in large sauce pan. Add and sauté:

2 cloves garlic, chopped

Add and bring to boil:

2 c. chicken broth

Add:

5 c. fresh pumpkin, pared and cut into one-inch cubes

Cook until transparent. Puree in blender.

—Sherry Holland
Caracas, Venezuela

Fruit Soup
Norway

Serves 6

Combine the following ingredients in saucepan with enough water to cover them well:

2 lbs. mixed dried fruit
1 c. raisins
½ c. pearl tapioca
1 c. grape juice
1 c. sugar
2 sticks cinnamon, broken into pieces

Simmer until fruit is done and mixture has thickened. If you like, you might leave the cinnamon sticks whole and remove them before serving. The soup can be served either warm or cold.

Lemon Grass Soup
Thailand

Serves 4–6

I enjoy trying out recipes from Thailand and found most of the ingredients for this soup at a Thai store in Harrisburg, Pennsylvania. I found lemon grass plants being sold in our local nursery. I planted one in my garden and it thrived....

—Ruth Zook
Mechanicsburg, PA

Boil over medium heat:
  3 c. water
Add and cook until meat is soft:
  1 root lemon grass, chopped in thin rings
  1–2 chili peppers, chopped
  ½ yellow onion, chopped
  1 c. meat (any kind you like: shrimp, chicken, fish, and even tofu if you are a vegetarian)
Add and simmer:
  1–2 large red tomatoes, chopped
  2 t. fish sauce
  2 T. lemon or lime juice
  ⅓ can straw mushrooms
  3–4 slices of ginger (Thai ginger is best)
Add before removing from heat:
  2 T. green onions, chopped
  2 Kafir lime leaves
  2 T. Chinese parsley, chopped

—Kathy Brubaker
Bangkok, Thailand

A Space to Hear God's Word

Theologically speaking, the purpose of hospitality is to prepare a welcoming space for encounters with God's word. It's not that God's word cannot be heard in barren, inhospitable places or circumstances. God is not so limited, but we are. God can speak in any situation, but we, frail creatures, cannot always hear. The Bible witnesses to the struggle of the Hebrews in the wilderness where they were so preoccupied with the lack of creature comforts that they constantly complained against God and Moses. To keep their attention, to keep them moving, to keep them faithful, God often prepared dinners of manna and quail. Only then, when fed, could they hear the word. So it is with us.

—Mary W. Anderson, "Christian Hospitality"
The Christian Century, July 1, 1998

Mulligatawny Soup
India

Serves 4

Sauté until golden brown (keep from burning):
>   3 T. oil
>   2 medium onions, finely chopped

Add and simmer for 20 minutes:
>   2 bay leaves
>   1 t. coriander
>   ¼ t. turmeric
>   ½ t. cumin
>   6 pepper corns
>   4 whole cloves
>   2 small pieces stick cinnamon
>   ½ t. salt
>   ¼ t. red pepper
>   1 T. curry powder
>   3 c. chicken broth or water

Add and continue heating:
>   2 cans cream of chicken soup

If desired add ½ c. cooked rice. Simmer for 15 minutes. Add lemon juice at serving time. Good for a light supper served with Indian bread (*chappatis*) or whole-wheat pita bread.

>   —*Kalini Mohmad*
>   *India*

Curry vendor in India.

Curry Soup
Norway

Karrisuppe
(KAHR-ee-SUP)

Serves 6

Variations of this soup are served throughout Scandinavia. Norwegians and Swedes use meat stock, while Danes prefer fish stock.

Melt **2 T. butter** in the bottom of a deep saucepan and gently sauté:

> **1 small onion, sliced**
> **1 clove garlic, crushed**
> **1 medium apple, peeled, cored, and finely grated**
> **pinch of thyme**

Gradually stir in:

> **½–1 t. curry powder**
> **2 T. flour (optional)**

Cook for 2–3 minutes, then gradually add:

> **9 c. meat or fish stock**

Simmer for another 3–4 minutes. Just before serving, stir in:

> **⅔ c. heavy cream**

Serve with hot French bread.

Fish and Almond Soup
Argentina

Serves 8–10

Cut into bite-sized pieces:

> **2 lbs. fillet red snapper or sole**
> **1 lb. raw shrimp, shelled and deveined**

Melt **3 T. butter** in a saucepan and sauté **1 c. chopped onion** for 10 minutes. Add:

> **8 c. chicken broth**
> **¼ lb. ham, finely chopped**

Bring to a boil, cover, and simmer over a medium heat for 10 minutes. Stir in:

> **½ c. raw rice**
> **1 t. salt**
> **½ t. freshly ground black pepper**
> **½ t. saffron**

Finally, add the fish, cover the saucepan, and cook over low heat for 20 minutes. Then add:

> **1 c. ground almonds**

Add the shrimp and cook 10 minutes longer. Taste for seasoning, then stir in:

> **3 T. minced parsley**
> **3 hardboiled egg yolks, chopped**

Cream of Lentil Soup
Russia

Serves 4

Put in a kettle and cover with water:

1¾ lbs. stewing beef
½ lb. ham
1 bunch parsley
salt and pepper to taste

Bring to a boil, then reduce heat and simmer for 1 hour, adding water as needed. Drain. Dice the ham, save the meat broth, and reserve beef for another meal. Rinse and strain:

¾ lb. lentils

Transfer to a pot along with:

1 carrot, sliced
1 medium onion, chopped
2 T. bread crumbs

Season with salt and pepper. Cover with water and bring to a boil. Skim the liquid and cover the pot. Cook until the lentils are tender (about 30 minutes). Press the vegetables through a sieve or puree them in a food processor, then return them to the liquid. Reheat puree and add the meat broth. Stir well and simmer until thick. Blend together:

2 egg yolks
½ c. heavy cream

Add these to the soup. Heat, but do not allow to boil again. Add the diced ham and 1 bunch dill, chopped.

Bold Hospitality

God can use people like you and me to touch lives. It doesn't matter if we rent or own a house or an apartment; our homes are an extension of ourselves. When we practice hospitality, we have the opportunity to touch lives in an intimate, personal way. Be bold: God has not only given you the roof over your head, but also will give you the love and wisdom needed to open your home to others.

With a little planning and preparation—and a good measure of prayer—you can be prepared to share your home with friends, neighbors, and even the strangers God may send your way.

—Kathy Chapman Sharp, "Christian Hospitality,"
Christian Single Magazine

Borscht
Russia

Serves 8

Place in a large soup kettle or Dutch oven and bring to a boil:

8 c. water
1 lb. beef shanks
5 peppercorns (whole)
2 bay leaves
1 t. salt
½ t. dry dill weed

Reduce heat, cover, and simmer for 1½ hours or until beef is tender. Meanwhile in a skillet, sauté 3 medium beets, peeled and shredded, in **1 T. vegetable oil** for 3 minutes. Stir in **2 t. white vinegar** and set aside.

Remove beef with a slotted spoon and allow it to cool. Remove meat from bones; discard bones. Cut meat into chunks and set aside.

Strain broth, discarding peppercorns and bay leaves. Skim fat. Add enough **water** to the broth to make 6 cups; return broth to kettle. Add:

2 medium potatoes, peeled and cubed
2 medium carrots, sliced
1 c. shredded cabbage
2 T. fresh parsley, minced

Then add the beets and bring to a boil. In a skillet, sauté **1 medium onion** (chopped) in **1 T. vegetable oil** for 5–7 minutes or until tender. Sprinkle with **1 T. all-purpose flour**; stir until blended. Whisk this mixture into the soup. Reduce heat, cover, and simmer for 30 minutes or until vegetables are tender. Add:

2 medium tomatoes, chopped

Process the soup in small batches in a blender or food processor; pour into large saucepan. Add the beef shanks and heat through. Garnish the soup with **½ c. sour cream.**

Bean Soup
Germany

Bohnensuppe
(BOHN-en-SOOP-ay)

Serves 6–8

Soak overnight in a large kettle:

> **1 lb. Great Northern beans,**
> **washed and sorted**
> **1 qt. cold water**

The next day, add:

> **1½ qt. cold water**
> **½ lb. bacon**

Set over moderately high heat and bring to a boil. Adjust heat so mixture bubbles very gently, cover, and cook for 1 hour. Then add:

> **½ lb. green beans, strung and washed,**
> **cut into small pieces**
> **2 large celery ribs, thinly sliced**
> **(include some tops)**
> **2 large carrots, peeled, cut into small pieces**
> **1 large leek, trimmed, washed, and**
> **thinly sliced**
> **1 large onion, peeled and coarsely chopped**
> **½ c. parsley, chopped**
> **¾ lb. potatoes, peeled and cut into**
> **small pieces**
> **1 T. dried marjoram leaf, crumbled**
> **1 t. dry thyme leaf, crumbled**
> **2 large whole bay leaves**

Cover the kettle again and simmer 1 hour. Melt **3 T. unsalted butter** in heavy 8" skillet over low heat, blend in **4 T. all-purpose flour,** and let it brown very slowly, stirring occasionally. Mix small amount of the hot soup liquid into browned flour mixture, stir well, then return it to the kettle. Add:

> **1 T. salt**
> **½ t. pepper**

Cook uncovered, stirring often, for 5 minutes. Remove the bay leaves, taste for salt and pepper, and season as needed. Ladle into soup plates and accompany with crusty chunks of Wheat Bread (see recipe).

Cream of Potato Soup
Germany

Kartoffelcreme-suppe
(KAR-tuff-el-krem-SOOP-ay)

Serves 4

Melt **2 T. unsalted margarine or butter** in a large, heavy saucepan over moderate heat. Add:

> **2 large yellow onions, peeled and thinly sliced**
> **1 small leek, trimmed, washed well, and thinly sliced**
> **1 small celery rib, thinly sliced**
> **2 thick slices bacon, halved crosswise**
> **1 t. dried marjoram leaf, crumbled**
> **1 t. dried thyme leaf, crumbled**
> **¼ t. freshly grated nutmeg**

Stir-fry for about 2 minutes until nicely glazed. Reduce heat to low, cover, and steam 15 minutes until onions are very limp. Remove and discard bacon. Raise heat to moderate and add:

> **1 lb. potatoes, peeled and thinly sliced**
> **1 qt. rich chicken broth (preferably homemade)**

Bring to simmer uncovered, then adjust the heat so that the broth bubbles gently. Cover and simmer 40 minutes until the potatoes are mushy. Remove pan from heat and cool soup, still uncovered, for 15 minutes.

Puree the soup mixture in two batches by blending in a food processor or electric blender at high speed for 1 minute. Return soup to pan, mix in **salt and pepper** to taste. Heat the soup uncovered to serving temperature, ladle into bowls, and sprinkle each portion with **2 T. snipped chives** for garnish.

Goulash Soup
Germany

Gulaschsuppe
(GOO-lash-SOOP-ay)

Serves 6–8

Melt **2 T. butter** in a large heavy kettle over high heat, then brown in two batches:

> **2 lbs. boneless beef chuck, cut into ½" cubes**

As beef browns, transfer with a slotted spoon to a large heat-proof bowl. Melt **1 T. butter** in the kettle, then add:

> **4 medium yellow onions, peeled and coarsely chopped**
> **1 large garlic clove, peeled and minced**

Stir-fry about 5 minutes until translucent. Return the beef to the kettle. If desired, add:

> **2 T. Hungarian sweet-rose paprika**
> **1 t. dried thyme, crumbled**

Mellow over moderate heat for about 1–2 minutes, stirring often. Add:

> **2 c. rich beef broth**
> **4 c. cold water**

Bring to a boil, then adjust the heat so the mixture simmers easily. Cover and cook 45 minutes. If desired, add:

> **4 medium potatoes, peeled and cut into ½" cubes**
> **1 lb. green beans, snipped and snapped into 1" lengths**

Cover again and simmer slowly 45 minutes longer or until the beef, potatoes, and beans are all tender. Smooth into the soup:

> **3 T. tomato paste**
> **½ t. salt**
> **½ t. freshly ground pepper**

Taste and adjust salt as needed. Ladle into heated soup plates and serve as a luxurious appetizer or even the main course of a luncheon meal.

Potato and Leek Soup
France

Potage Parmentier
(poh-TAGE par-men-tee-AY)

Serves 6–8

This soup is usually served with traditional French bread, and when served cold it is called vichyssoise.

Combine in saucepan and cover:

> 3 medium potatoes, peeled and sliced ⅛" thick
> 3 medium leeks, washed thoroughly and sliced ⅛" thick
> 3 10¾-oz. cans chicken broth
> 1 broth can of cold water

Bring to a boil over medium-high heat. Reduce heat and simmer 35–45 minutes or until vegetables are tender. Without draining off broth, mash vegetables in the saucepan with a potato masher until they are fairly smooth. (If they will not mash easily, soup has not cooked long enough. Let simmer 10–15 minutes longer.) Add:

> ½ c. whipping cream (add up to an extra ½ c. milk if you like thin soup)
> 2 T. butter or margarine
> 2 t. salt
> ¼ t. pepper

Heat the soup just to the boiling point. (Do not boil.) Sprinkle each serving with chives.

Onion Tomato Soup
France

Serves 6

Sauté in a large saucepan until tender:

> 4 c. thinly sliced onions
> 1 garlic clove, minced
> 2 T. butter or margarine

Then add:

> 46-oz. can tomato juice
> 2 t. beef bouillon granules
> 3 T. lemon juice
> 2 t. dried parsley flakes
> 2 t. brown sugar

Bring to a boil, then reduce heat and simmer uncovered for 10 minutes, stirring occasionally. Ladle soup into oven-proof soup bowls. Top with **6 slices French bread**; sprinkle with **2 c. shredded mozzarella cheese**. Heat under broiler until the cheese bubbles.

Minestrone
Italy

Serves 4

Melt **4 T. butter** and heat **4 T. vegetable oil** in stock pot. Pierce 1 clove garlic and sauté in the pot for 5 minutes. Remove garlic. Add:

1 large yellow onion, minced

Sauté until tender. Add:

> **2 small cans tomato sauce**
> **2–3 chicken bouillon cubes**
> **dash of basil, parsley, and oregano**
> **8-oz. can red kidney beans**
> **½ c. chopped parsley**

Simmer 10 minutes. Add:

> **4–5 celery ribs, sliced**
> **1 potato, diced**
> **4–5 carrots, sliced**
> **enough water to cover**

Cover pot and let simmer 10 minutes. Then add:

> **1 bunch Swiss chard, coarsely chopped**

Simmer 30 minutes or until all vegetables are al dente. Season to taste. For low cholesterol, substitute polyunsaturated vegetable oil for butter.

—*Shirley DeFeudis Taylor*

Blessed in Receiving

Hospitality includes receiving. When we are the recipients—when we stay with relatives, for example, we are called to practice another sort of hospitality: to receive with humility, gratitude, and an uncritical spirit what is offered in love—to remember that we are to receive every good thing as from the hand of God. To consider hospitality in this way is to recognize that it always involves exchange—and that we are never in a position to calculate the final value of what is given and what is received. Portia's words about the quality of mercy apply also to this virtue, rightly exercised: "It blesseth him that gives and him that takes."

—Marilyn Chandler McEntyre,
"My House, God's House,"
Christianity Today, April 23, 2001

Wedding Soup
Italy

Serves 6

Heat to boiling:

3 qts. chicken stock (see below)
1 T. Italian seasoning
salt and pepper to taste

Add:

1 c. fettuccine, broken into 1" pieces

Cook until pasta is done. Drop into 6 heated soup bowls:

30 small broiled meatballs

Top bowls with boiling soup, sprinkle with fresh chopped chives or cooked spinach leaves. Serve with Parmesan cheese and hot crusty Italian bread.

Chicken Stock

5 lbs. chicken backs and necks
4 qts. cold water
½ lb. carrots, diced large
2 bay leaves
½ lb. onions, diced large
2 stalks celery, cut into 2" pieces
2 sprigs parsley

Place all ingredients in large stock pot, cover with cold water. Bring to boil, cover, reduce heat to a slow simmer, and simmer for 4–5 hours. Strain through colander, chill, and skim off fat. Can be refrigerated for 3–4 days or frozen.

Our Eternal Home

Let's be generous in this life, knowing our true reward will be to enjoy God's perfect hospitality in our eternal home.

—Keith D. Wright
Evangelical Visitor, Feb. 1996, p. 6.

Lentil Soup
Italy

Serves 5

In large saucepan, heat **1 T. olive oil** and then lightly sauté for about 5 minutes:

> **1 c. sliced carrots**
> **½ c. sliced celery**
> **⅓ c. chopped onion**

or until vegetables are crisp-tender. Stir in:

> **5 c. water**
> **½ small head cabbage, cored and cut into 1" pieces (4 c.)**
> **1 c. dry lentils, rinsed and drained**
> **1 c. tomato puree**
> **1½ t. sugar**
> **½ t. dried oregano, crushed**
> **1½ t. salt**
> **¼ t. pepper**

Bring to boil; reduce heat. Cover and simmer about 45 minutes or until lentils are very soft.

Riding a gondola on the canals of Venice, Italy. Photo © Jack Hollingsworth/Corbis.

Roasted Peanuts
Zambia

Musuka
(Moo-soo-kah)

Serves 6

Roast at 350° for 20–25 minutes until slightly brown, stirring frequently:

>   2 c. raw peanuts

Combine and pour over hot peanuts:

>   ¾ t. salt
>   1 c. water

Continue roasting peanuts until moisture is absorbed. Serve as a snack or at the end of a meal as a dessert.

—Shelly Muleya, Mizinga Village
Choma, Zambia

Argentine Chicken and Vegetable Soup
Argentina

Sopa Criolla de Pollo
(SOAP-uh cree-O-la day POH-yo)

Serves 4–6

Combine in a saucepan:

>   4-lb. chicken, disjointed
>   5 c. water
>   ½ c. chopped onions
>   2 T. diced green peppers
>   ½ c. peeled, diced tomatoes
>   2 cloves garlic, minced
>   ½ c. diced carrots

Bring to boil. Cover and cook over low heat 1¼ hours. Add:

>   1 T. salt
>   ½ t. white pepper
>   ½ c. raw rice
>   ½ c. diced potatoes
>   ½ c. shredded cabbage
>   ½ c. green peas
>   2 T. minced parsley
>   1 T. minced cilantro or fresh coriander
>   (optional)

Simmer for 30 minutes. Taste for seasoning and serve in deep bowls. The meat can be cut from the bones before serving, if you like.

Chicken Soup
Brazil

Canja
(KAHN-ya)

Serves 6–8

Place **1 stewing chicken** in large saucepan and cover with **2 qt. water**. Add:

1 lb. onions
2 carrots
1 lb. fresh, ripe tomatoes or 16-oz. can whole tomatoes
2 stalks celery, sliced
small bunch of fresh cilantro or parsley, chopped
3–4 celery leaves
12 black peppercorns
1 t. salt

Bring to boil, skimming off the foam that comes to surface. Turn heat down and simmer for 2 hours. Remove chicken from broth and, when cool enough to handle, remove and discard skin. Pull meat from bones and cut into strips. Strain broth, discard vegetables (which have already passed on their goodness to the broth), and return chicken meat to saucepan along with:

½ c. long-grain white rice
2 carrots

Bring back to boil, then reduce heat and simmer for another 30 minutes. Season to taste.

Avocado Dip
Argentina

Makes about 2 cups

Cut **2 avocados** in half lengthwise and scoop out pulp. Chop fine, then blend with:

4 anchovies, minced
4 T. green onions, minced
1½ T. lime or lemon juice
¼ t. Tabasco® sauce

Taste for seasoning.

Soft Pretzels
Germany

Makes 12 pretzels

Dissolve in **1½ c. water**:
> **2 packets of yeast**

Add:
> **2 t. salt**
> **4 c. unsifted bread flour**

Mix ingredients together, knead briefly, and form into a ball. Cover with a damp cloth and allow to rest 15 minutes. In a small bowl dissolve:
> **3 c. baking soda**
> **1 c. cool water**

(The soda will not totally dissolve, therefore needs to be stirred occasionally.) Divide dough into 12 equal pieces and roll into 8 ropes.

Soak two at a time in baking soda water for 1–2 minutes. Pat lightly with paper towel and shape on greased baking sheet (5–6 per sheet). Sprinkle with **coarse salt** as desired. Bake at 350° for 20 minutes.

> —*Faithe Hoffman*
> *Palmyra, PA*

Avocado Whip
Brazil

Abacate Batida
(ah-bah-CAH-tay bah-TEE-dah)

Serves 4

Remove peel and pit from **1 avocado**. Mash through a sieve. Add:
> **juice of 1 lime**
> **2 T. sugar**

Combine this mixture with:
> **1 c. vanilla ice cream**

Beat with rotary beater until smooth. Place in freezing tray and chill, *but do not freeze.*

The German autobahn passes fertile farmland. Photo © Corbis.

Salties
Nepal

Nimki
(NIM-kee)

Serves 12–15

Using a pastry blender, mix as for pastry:

2 c. whole wheat flour
2 T. cumin seed, ground
2 T. onion salt
½ t. salt
4 T. oil

Knead thoroughly until elastic. Divide into 56 balls. Flour a pastry board and roll out dough. Cut in strips diagonally ¾" wide.

Deep-fry until golden brown at a temperature of 350°. Lift from hot oil and dry on paper towels. Salt to taste. Cool and eat as a snack.

—*Esther Lenhert*
Kathmandu, Nepal

Vegetable Fritters
India

Pakoras
(pa-IKOR-ahs)

Serves 6

Sift:
>**2 c. besan (ground lentils) flour**
>**3 t. baking powder**

Add:
>**2 t. turmeric**
>**1 t. coriander powder**
>**2 t. red ground chili**
>**salt to taste**

Gradually add water to make a batter. To batter add:
>**2 medium onions, chopped**

Drop by teaspoonful into hot fat or vegetable oil and deep-fry until crisp. Potatoes, eggplant, cauliflower or spinach, cut in small pieces, may also be used. Dip into batter and deep fry.

—*Kas Bert*
Carlisle, PA

Fried Pork Bits
Argentina

Carnitas
(car-NEAT-ahs)

Makes about 3 dozen

Cut **2 lbs. fat pork** into bite-size pieces. Combine in a skillet with:
>**1½ c. water**
>**2 t. salt**
>**¼ t. ground cumin**
>**½ t. dried ground chili peppers**

Bring to boil, cover, and cook over high heat until water evaporates. Remove cover and cook pork until browned and crisp. Pierce with mini-forks and serve with a spicy sauce as dip, if desired.

Salads, Dressings, and Relishes

Hospitality in Italy

Italians eat their serious meals in courses and (usually) insist on clean plates with each course. The first is *antipasti* or hors d'oeuvre; then the *minestra* or soup (see recipe). Then comes the official first course or *primi piatta*, usually a rice or pasta dish; this is perhaps the largest dish of the meal and is followed by the *secondi piatta*, a meat course with several vegetables, all smaller portions.

Following this is the *insalata* (salad), with *formaggio* (cheese) or *dolci* (sweets of some sort). The meal is ended with the *frutta*. If the occasion demands a more elaborate meal, sorbets, quiches, or soufflés are often added, usually between the main (*piatta*) courses.

"Italian cooking" usually calls up visions of huge stacks of spaghetti, thick pizzas, and pungently scented ravioli, all smothered in tomato sauce. But each geographical region adds its own special refinements and variations to that cuisine.

"Pasta is a staple in the Italian diet," reports Krista Huck, who with her husband and girls spent a term as missionaries in Italy. "It does not take long before discovering that there are many ways to fix pasta, but only one way to cook it: *Al dente* ('just done,' or 'just finished'). The greatest sin in Italian cooking is to overcook the pasta."

Typical Italian meals in homes often last for hours, and this is an understandable outgrowth of the Italian reverence for the family. Sunday afternoon meals together with the entire family are common. The traditional Sunday meal starts with pasta, many times featuring noodles home made the night before. (See Krista's recipe for Broccoli Pasta.) After that, new plates appear for the meat and vegetables. Then come courses of salad, and then a fruit course, many times including fresh fruit from nearby orchards. The courses are brought out separately and leisurely, allowing lots of time for fellowship, for exchanging news and opinions, for just getting closer together as a family.

Such grand feasts close with the family specialty: some kind of Italian pastry, served with a cup of Italian espresso. Often guests will bring trays of their special pastries as favors for the hostess.

One person who had lived in Italy for some time reports: "Most people over there are still functioning on an agricultural schedule. Lunch is late: 1:00 in the afternoon and some times later. This is the largest meal of the day, perhaps a tradition coming from times when farmers needed strength to get them through their long day out of doors. After lunch is rest time for some of the afternoon, and many stores in smaller towns close between 1:00 and 4:00 or so each day. At 8:00 or so there is a light dinner before bedtime."

Tamaulipeca Salad
Mexico

Ensalada
Tamaulipeca
(En-sah-LAH-dah
tah-mow-lee-PAY-kah)

Serves 6

Mix together well:
> 4–6 carrots, grated
> 4 apples, peeled and cubed
> 1–2 c. pineapple, drained and cubed
> 1 c. mayonnaise
> ½ c. raisins
> pineapple juice as desired

—*Gracely Vázquez Espinosa*
Ciudad Victoria
Tamps, Mexico

Avocado Salad
Argentina

Ensalada de
Aguacate
(en-sah-LAH-dah day
ah-gwah-KAHT-ay)

Serves 6

Beat together:
> ½ c. olive oil
> ¼ c. vinegar
> 1 t. salt
> ½ t. black pepper
> ½ t. dry mustard
> 1 clove garlic, minced

Cut in half lengthwise:
> 3 avocados

Remove pits. Prick flesh of avocados in several places. Pour the dressing into the avocado halves and sprinkle with:
> ½ c. chopped pimientos

Serve on lettuce.

Chayote Salad with Oranges
Brazil

Salada de Xuxu
(su-LAH-dah day ZOO-ZOO)

Serves 4

Chayote (chah-YOH-teh) squash is common in Latin America and can be found in most large markets. North Americans also call it "vegetable squash," and the French call it christophene.

Mix in a large salad bowl:
> **2 chayotes, peeled, skinned, shredded on grater**
> **3 oranges, peeled, sectioned (juice reserved)**
> **bunch of scallions, white parts only, chopped**

In a separate bowl, make a dressing of:
> **1 T. extra virgin olive oil**
> **juice of 2 limes**
> **reserved orange juice**
> **sea salt and freshly ground pepper**

Add dressing to the salad and mix well. Chill for at least 30 minutes. Toss once more to mingle the flavors thoroughly, then serve with herbs (chopped fresh cilantro, parsley, or mint) sprinkled on top.

Hand-painted plates on display in Sidi Bou Said, Tunisia. Photo © Larry Lee/ Corbis.

Greek Salad

In large bowl, mix:

1 small head lettuce, torn into bite-size pieces
3 medium tomatoes, cut up
¾ c. black olives, pits removed and sliced
in halves
1 medium onion, sliced in rings
½ small head of cauliflower, cut into
bite-size pieces

Mix:

1 c. plain nonfat yogurt
1 T. olive oil
2 T. lemon juice
1 t. oregano
1½ t. dry mustard
½ t. salt
¼ t. black pepper

Toss with vegetables. Sprinkle with pepper. Chill.

—Beulah Heisey
Mechanicsburg, PA

Salada la Valenciana
Spain

Serves 6

Combine in salad bowl and toss thoroughly:

1 thick slice French bread, rubbed with 1 large
garlic clove and broken into pieces
Romaine lettuce, broken into bite-size pieces
3 large oranges, peeled and sectioned
4-oz. can pimentos, cut in strips
1 medium onion, thinly sliced
10–12 pimento-stuffed olives
¼ c. olive oil

Add and toss again:

salt and pepper
2 T. red wine vinegar

—Merly Bundy
Madrid, Spain

Basic French Green Salad
France

La Salade Verte a la Francaise

(lah sa-LAHD VER-tay ah lah fran-SEZ)

Serves 4–5

Trim **2 small heads fresh Bibb lettuce**. Pull leaves apart, inspecting them for dirt, damage, etc., and wash well under cold running water. Soak greens in very cold water for 5 minutes, sprinkling them with **1 T. salt**. Rinse greens again in cold running water, drain, and pat dry with paper towels. Rub inside of salad bowl with:

   1 small garlic clove, cut in half

Then discard garlic. Pour into bowl:

   ¼ cup vinaigrette dressing (use bottled or see recipe below)

Pile the dried lettuce leaves on top. When ready to serve, toss greens in the vinaigrette, making sure all leaves are coated with dressing. Serve at once.

Variations: Any favorite greens may be substituted for the lettuce. Also, French cooks love to add walnut halves. Boil the nuts for 7 minutes in salted water, rinse, and scrub them clean. Then line bottom of bowl with them, making sure they get well distributed when the greens are tossed.

Vinaigrette Dressing
France

Makes 4–5 servings

Chop **1 clove garlic** into very fine pieces and put in a small bowl. Use the back of a spoon to mash garlic, then mix it with **½ t. salt**. Add:

   3 T. red wine vinegar

   ¼ t. pepper

Stir ingredients until smooth. Place in small jar with tight-fitting lid. Add:

   6 T. olive or vegetable oil

Close the jar and shake until well blended.

Tuscan Bread Salad
Italy

Serves 6

In a large bowl, stir together:
- **3 c. dry Italian bread cubes**
- **2 large ripe tomatoes, peeled and coarsely chopped**
- **1 small red onion, chopped**
- **⅓ c. sliced, pitted ripe olives**
- **¼ c. chopped fresh basil or oregano leaves**

In a screw-top jar, combine:
- **3 T. olive oil**
- **2 T. red wine vinegar**
- **3 cloves garlic, finely chopped**
- **¼ t. salt**
- **⅛ t. pepper**

Close the jar and shake dressing until well blended. Pour over bread mixture. Serve immediately on lettuce leaves.

Cabbage Slaw for Freezer
United States / Pennsylvania Dutch

Mix and let stand for 1 hour:
- **1 medium head cabbage, shredded**
- **1 t. salt**

Combine for dressing:
- **1 c. vinegar**
- **¼ c. water**
- **2 c. sugar**
- **1 t. mustard seed**
- **1 t. celery seed**

Boil the dressing for 1 minute, then cool. At the end of the hour, squeeze excess moisture out of the cabbage. Add:
- **1 green pepper, chopped**
- **1 carrot, grated**
- **1 c. celery, chopped**

Then add cooled dressing and mix well. Put in containers and freeze. This slaw can be refrozen.

—Anna Ruth Ressler
Elizabethtown, PA

Cabbage Relish

United States / Pennsylvania Dutch

Makes 5–6 pints

Grind with food grinder or food processor (using the 1-star blade):

1 large cabbage
4 green peppers
5 medium carrots
6 onions

Mix with ¼ c. salt and let stand for 2 hours. Drain well. Add:

3 c. sugar
1½ pt. cider vinegar
½ T. celery seed
½ T. mustard seed

Mix well. Pack in pint jars and store in refrigerator. Keeps for at least 6 months. Serve with beef, pork, ham loaf, or hamburgers.

—Kathryn Light
Palmyra, PA

Pumpkin Cabbage Salad

Japan

Serves 6

Mix and set aside for 12 hours:

2 c. cabbage, chopped
½–1 t. salt

Cook **2 c. squash or pumpkin (cubed)** until crisp-tender, then cool. At the end of two hours, squeeze excess moisture out of the cabbage. Mix cabbage and squash with enough **mayonnaise** to hold together. Serve chilled.

—Mariko Kogoma
Tokyo, Japan

Cucumber Salad
Norway

Agurksalat
(ag-GURK-sal-at)

Serves 6

Wash **1 cucumber** and slice very thin, using vegetable slicer, so that slices are almost transparent. Place in deep bowl and sprinkle with **salt**. Cover with plate and weigh down with heavy object. Leave for 12 hours. Drain thoroughly, then rinse off the salt and squeeze out the remaining juice. Boil in a saucepan:

> **scant ½ c. water**
> **½ t. salt**
> **pinch white pepper**

Let cool and add:

> **scant ½ c. white wine vinegar or juice of one**
> **lemon**
> **sugar to taste (about 3 T.)**

When dressing is cold, pour it over the cucumber and chill for half an hour. Just before serving, sprinkle with chopped parsley or dill. Serve cucumber salad with roast chicken or other roast meat.

Beet Salad
Russia

Serves 4–6

Grate together in a large salad bowl:

> **3–4 medium beets, cooked**
> **2 medium raw apples, cored and peeled**

Add:

> **2 tsp. chopped walnuts**
> **2–3 cloves of crushed garlic**
> **2–3 T. mayonnaise**

—Mary Faducovich Hart

Mayonnaise with Herbs
Russia

Excellent with cold, steamed or boiled fish. Many Russian chefs prefer this as a dressing for potato salad.

Rub through fine sieve:
  yolks of 2 hard-boiled eggs
Mix until smooth with:
  1 t. salt
  ½ t. pepper
  1 t. sugar
  1 t. dry mustard
Gradually stir in:
  1½ c. sour cream
Begin stirring in, drop by drop:
  3 T. olive oil
The mixture must be quite thick by the time all the oil has been added. Then add:
  1 t. lemon juice
  1 t. vinegar
This forms the basic Russian mayonnaise. Now add the herbs:
  1 T. minced chives
  1 t. minced tarragon
  1 t. minced chervil
  1 t. minced sour gherkins
  1 t. minced celery
  1 T. minced dill pickle

Rice and Raisin Salad
South Africa

Serves 8

A nice change from the usual cole slaw, as rice gives the cabbage a milder flavor.

Place in a large bowl and mix well, adding mayonnaise last:
  3 c. cooked rice, cooled
  1 small cabbage, grated
  1 green pepper, diced
  1 medium onion, diced
  ½ c. raisins
  1 c. mayonnaise

—Rosina Madlabane
Soshanguve, South Africa

Cold Potato Salad
Sweden

Potatissallad
(po-taty-sal-AD)

Serves 4

Arrange in a serving bowl that has been rubbed with a clove of garlic:
>   6–8 medium-sized, cooked potatoes, peeled and diced

Sprinkle on top:
>   2 T. finely chopped parsley and tarragon

Add:
>   1–2 T. capers
>   1–2 T. chopped chives

Mix the vinegar, oil, salt, and pepper in a tumbler:
>   1½–2 T. wine vinegar
>   5–6 T. olive or salad oil
>   1 t. salt
>   ¼ t. ground white pepper

Shake the dressing well before pouring it over the ingredients in the bowl. Allow the potato salad to chill in refrigerator for several hours. Just before serving, garnish with capers and sliced raw leek, chopped chives, or parsley.

Rice Salad
Québec

Salade de riz
(sa-LAHD doh REE)

Serves 6

Mix together:
>   ¾ c. mayonnaise
>   6 t. lemon juice
>   ¾ t. curry powder
>   1 t. onion, finely chopped
>   ¼ t. dry mustard
>   salt and pepper to taste

Add:
>   3 c. rice, cooked and cooled
>   1½ c. celery, chopped
>   1½ c. cooked ham, cut into small cubes
>   ¾ c. crushed pineapple, drained

Chill 4–6 hours. Serve the chilled salad on lettuce. Brown rice makes a tasty substitute for white rice.

—*Lucie Boulanger*
Romuald, Québec

White Bean Salad
Italy

Serves 4–6

Rinse and soak overnight:

1 lb. dried white navy beans

Drain, pour into large saucepan, and cover with fresh water. Add:

1 small onion, cut into chunks
1 carrot, thickly sliced
1 stalk celery with leaves, cut in large pieces
1 whole bay leaf
2 cloves garlic, crushed but not separated
1 large twig each of fresh rosemary, sage, and thyme
1 T. olive oil

Bring to simmer and cook 45 minutes. Add more water or a splash of broth if necessary. Cook until just tender, about 15–20 minutes more. Drain, then remove vegetables and herbs. Toss with:

2 T. each of fresh thyme, sage, and rosemary leaves
3–4 T. extra-virgin olive oil
salt and pepper to taste

Pasta Salad
Italy

Serves 6

Cook ¾ c. spiral pasta according to package directions; rinse with cold water and drain. Place in large salad bowl. Add:

1½ c. halved cherry tomatoes
1 c. sliced fresh mushrooms
¼ c. chopped sweet red pepper
¼ c. chopped green pepper
3 T. thinly sliced green onions
1½ c. zesty Italian salad dressing

Cover and refrigerate for at least 4 hours or overnight, then drain. In a separate bowl, combine:

¾ c. mayonnaise
½ c. grated Parmesan cheese

Stir in:

⅓ c. Provolone cheese
2¼-oz. can sliced olives

Gently fold this dressing into the chilled pasta. Serve in lettuce-lined bowl if desired.

Macaroni Salad with Hot Dressing
Germany

Serves 6

Drain a **3-oz. can sliced mushrooms**, reserving liquid; add enough water to the reserved portion to make 1 cup. In a 3-qt. saucepan, fry until crisp:

5 strips of bacon

Drain, reserving drippings. Crumble bacon and set aside. Combine in a bowl:

½ c. sugar
3 T. all-purpose flour
½ t. salt
⅛ t. pepper

Blend this mixture into the reserved bacon drippings and add to saucepan. Combine in a bowl:

⅓ c. vinegar
reserved cup of mushroom liquid

Add to flour mixture; cook and stir until thickened and bubbly. Meanwhile cook:

3 oz. macaroni

Follow package directions and drain. In saucepan, lightly toss the macaroni with dressing, mushrooms, and bacon. Add:

½ c. chopped celery
½ c. chopped green onions

Garnish with radishes and parsley if desired.

Row houses on the waterfront in Copenhagen, Denmark. Photo © Corbis.

Husum Shrimp Salad
Germany

Husumer Krabbensalat
(hue-SUE-mer krab-BEN-sahl-ad)

Serves 6

Lightly toss together in a medium-size bowl:
- **½ lb. small shrimp, cooked, shelled, and deveined**
- **1 c. green beans, cooked and drained**
- **2 extra-large hard-boiled eggs, peeled and coarsely chopped**
- **2 T. minced parsley**
- **1 T. finely snipped fresh chives**
- **2 T. finely snipped fresh dill**

Combine in a 2-cup measure:
- **½ c. mayonnaise**
- **1 T. Dijon mustard**
- **⅛ t. salt**
- **⅛ t. freshly ground black pepper**
- **¼ c. heavy cream, whipped to stiff peaks**
- **1 T. freshly squeezed lemon juice**

Pour half of this dressing over salad, cover, and refrigerate for at least 1 hour. Also cover and refrigerate the remaining dressing. Just before serving, toss salad well, adding a little more dressing if necessary. Also taste for salt and pepper and add more if needed. Serve the extra dressing on the side.

Shrimp Salad
Denmark

Rejesalat
(RAY-sal-at)

Serves 6

Season **½ c. mayonnaise** with **2–3 T. grape juice**, and carefully stir in:
- **⅓ lb. cooked, peeled shrimp**
- **⅔ c. fresh mushrooms, trimmed and sliced**
- **¾ c. cooked asparagus, cut into 1-inch pieces**

Arrange on serving pate. Garnish with mustard and cress or with a few extra shrimp.

Variations: Crab or lobster may be used instead of shrimp, making this *krabbesalat* or *hummersalat* in Danish. To cut calories, substitute vinaigrette dressing for the juice and mayonnaise and serve on lettuce, omitting the mustard and cress.

Shrimp Salad
Argentina

Salada de
Camaroes
(sa-LAH-dah dah
kah-mah-ROWS)

Serves 6

Toss together:
 1 lb. shrimp, cooked, cleaned, and chopped
 2 avocados, peeled and diced
 2 T. lemon juice
 ½ c. mayonnaise
Taste for seasoning, adding salt and pepper if needed.
Heap on lettuce leaves and place spoonful of mayonnaise
on top. Sprinkle with **2 hard-boiled eggs,** chopped.

Fish Salad
Argentina

Ensalada de
Pescado
(en-sah-LAH-dah
day
pess-KAH-doh)

Serves 6–8

Combine in a 2-qt. saucepan:
 ½ lb. white fish
 1 onion, cut into fourths
 3 c. water
 2 teaspoons salt
 ¼ t. white pepper
Bring to boil and cook over low heat for 25 minutes.
Drain well, flake, and cool. Toss together with:
 ½ c. thinly sliced green onions
 1 c. chopped celery
 ¾ c. diced tomatoes
 ¼ c. minced green peppers
 ¼ c. chopped, stuffed olives
 1 t. salt
 ¼ t. white pepper
Fold in mayonnaise. Serve on watercress or lettuce.

Fresh Tomato Chutney
India

Tamatar Chatni
(Ta-MA-tar CHAT nee)

Serves 8-10

Chop:
> **1 lb. tomatoes**
> **1 large onion**

Add and mix well:
> **2 dashes Tabasco® sauce**
> **¼ t. each salt and pepper**
> **½ t. sugar**
> **½ t. garlic powder**
> **dash of vinegar**

Add:
> **1 t. oil from mango pickle (or mustard or vegetable oil)**

—*A. J. Mann*
Bihar, India

Taubolleh
Jordan

(Tah-BOO-lee)

Taubolleh *is usually eaten by scooping it up with a lettuce leaf, cabbage leaf, or grape leaf.*

Soak in **2 c. of water** until soft (about 2 hours):
> **1 c. bulgur wheat (medium crushed wheat)**

Drain off excess water. Combine in a bowl with the drained bulgur:
> **1½ c. parsley, chopped very fine**
> **1 green onion, chopped in small pieces**
> **½ c. mint leaves, chopped very fine**

Combine and pour into the bulgur mixture, mixing well:
> **1 c. olive oil**
> **2 t. salt**
> **½ c. lemon juice**

Add:
> **1 small tomato, chopped**

Variations:
Reduce or increase the amount of oil as desired. Use less parsley. Add cucumber and garbanzo beans.

—*Ethel Kreider*
Lancaster, PA

Orange Chutney
India

(CHUT-nee)

Makes about 4 cups

Mix together in a bowl:
> **4 oranges, peeled, diced, and seeded**
> **1 onion, minced**
> **½ c. grated coconut**
> **1 T. mint leaves, crushed**

Cover and chill in refrigerator. Serve as an accompaniment to curry.

—Ken Hoke
Carlisle, PA (Bihar, India)

Raita
India

(RIE-tah)

Makes about 4 cups

Peel, grate and set aside for 1 hour:
> **2 cucumbers**

Mix:
> **1 medium onion, chopped fine**
> **½ t. ground cumin**
> **1 pt. yogurt**
> **½ t. salt**

Drain all water off cucumbers and add the yogurt mixture. Serve as an accompaniment to curry.

—Ken Hoke
Carlisle, PA (Bihar, India)

Tomato Chutney
India

(CHUT-nee)

Delicious with curries or as an accompaniment to any meat dish. Makes a nice hostess gift when sealed in a small jar and topped with a bow!

Grind in a blender:
  1 lb. onions
  2 oz. garlic
  4 oz. fresh ginger
  1 hot red pepper
In large kettle, mix the above ingredients together with:
  4 lbs. tomatoes, peeled and chopped
  ¾ c. slivered and blanched almonds
  4 c. sugar
  2 c. vinegar
  2 t. salt
Cook, stirring frequently until the mixture reaches the desired consistency (thick and syrupy). Toward end of cooking time, add:
  1½ c. raisins
Seal in small canning jars.

Variations: Use less ginger and pepper.

—*Leora Yoder*
Mechanicsburg, PA (Bihar, India)

Oriental Salad Dressing
Japan

This dressing can be used on a variety of salad ingredients, including chilled Chinese noodles.

Combine equal parts of:
  sesame oil
  vinegar
  soy sauce

—*Mariko Kogoma*
Tokyo, Japan

Vegetables

Hospitality in France

For the French, there are two distinctly different cooking styles: one is grand, fancy, rich, and complicated (*haute cuisine*); the other is simple, everyday fare (*cuisine bourgeois*). The first type of cooking is found in the homes of the wealthy and in highly touted restaurants; the second is the norm in small "family" restaurants or in the private homes of millions of wonderful family cooks.

Through the years the wealthy in France were provided with chefs, expensive equipment, and developed lavish customs. Common people found ways to use a fireplace or a woodstove to produce equally delicious fair. If French cooking can be called an art, *haute cuisine* dining in that country should be termed a ceremony. The eating of a well-prepared meal is considered one of the perfect pleasures of life: gracious, bountiful, leisurely . . . and expensive.

In French restaurants in America, two items consistently are presented. Both are simple, ageless recipes coming from the seacoast homes and restaurants of France. One is *bouillabaisse* (literally "bubbles and settle"), a soup made of fishermen's leftovers. The other is *mariniere*: shellfish cooked with fish stock, as barge workers have done it for centuries. Both are really very simple fare, but easily adapted to provide a fancy art form.

The omelet is considered by connoisseurs to be the most glorious achievement of French egg cooking. The French didn't invent the dish, but perfected it through the ages. Interestingly enough, French cooks insist that the French omelet is the simplest way for French chefs to fix eggs.

One knowledgeable Frenchman says that the overwhelming favorite lunch for office workers is *steak frites salade verte fromage* (grilled beefsteak, French fries, salad, and cheese). He also says that many French chefs today tenderize the meat by beating it with the edge of a small dinner plate, just as they did a hundred years ago. (See recipe for Grilled Steak French Style.)

In France, rice pudding is mother's remedy for anything that ails the family, much as chicken soup has been for Jewish mothers. Rice pudding has numberless variations. Children seek it as they come home from school; Granddad brightens when he raids the refrigerator at midnight and finds it there. Mom rejoices, since it's one of France's most economical desserts.

Fast fading in France is the traditional custom of shopping for the day's food at the local market. For years it has been the custom of housewives to spend their mornings drifting from shop to shop, winding their way among the street venders. Both buyers and sellers will discuss food and its preparation with great enthusiasm until it's time for the street merchants to close their stalls at noon.

Mushrooms with Peanut Butter
Zimbabwe

Serves 6

Cook together:
4 c. fresh mushrooms, washed and sliced
½ c. water
½ t. salt
Set mushrooms aside. Add to the water in which mushrooms were cooked:
½ c. peanut butter
Cook until thickened. Add the cooked mushrooms and simmer a few minutes longer. Serve with thick corn meal porridge or rice.

—Abbie Dube
Bulawayo, Zimbabwe

Creamed Mushrooms
Norway

Soppstuing
(SOAP-stewing)

Serves 4

Sauté in **2 T. butter** for a few minutes:
1 lb. mushrooms, cleaned and sliced
Add:
salt to taste
lemon juice to taste
Finally, stir in:
generous 1 c. heavy cream
Cook for 3–5 minutes. Serve hot as a filling in an omelet, in pastry shells, or on buttered toast.

Mushrooms Grilled with Garlic and Parsley
France

Les Champignons Grilles à la Florentine
(luh sham-peen-YON GREEL-sa-la fla-ren-TINE)

Serves 4

French chefs serve this as a luncheon main dish on a bed of vermicelli, along with a green salad, apples, and cheese.

Select:
> **8–12 very large, fresh domestic mushrooms**

Wipe mushrooms clean with soft, damp cloth and carefully pare away stem ends. Drive point of sharp paring knife into the caps of the mushrooms several times and push into incisions:
> **2 plump cloves of garlic, cut lengthwise into tiny, pointed spikes**

Brush mushrooms thoroughly with **3 T. olive oil**. Line a baking tin with aluminum foil, set mushrooms on it, and grill them under a hot broiler. Turn mushrooms once, return to broiler. Remove to warm dish and sprinkle them with:
> **½ t. leaf thyme**
> **2 T. finely chopped parsley**
> **salt and pepper to taste**

Serve as they are or with pasta, providing salt and pepper for those wishing to heighten taste.

A floating vegetable vendor in Bangkok, Thailand. Photo © Corbis.

Salsa
Spain

Gazpacho
(Gahth-PAH-choh)

Serves 8

Gazpacho is traditionally served with small bowls of raw vegetables and garlic croutons.

Chop in electric blender:
    6 large ripe tomatoes
    1 small clove garlic
Add to above mixture and blend again:
    ½ onion
    ¼ green pepper
    ½ cucumber
Strain mixture into tureen or serving bowl and chill in refrigerator. Before serving, blend the following ingredients and add to the first mixture:
    6 T. olive oil
    4 T. lemon juice
    salt and pepper to taste
    1½ c. tomato juice

—Merly Bundy
Madrid, Spain

Hominy in Peanut Butter Sauce
Zimbabwe

Serves 2–4

Heat:
    16-oz. can hominy, undrained
Add slowly and mix well:
    ¼ c. peanut butter
Simmer on very low heat for several minutes. May be served as the main course of a meal.

—Beatrice Ncube
Dekezi, Zimbabwe

Tomato-Onion Relish
Honduras

Chilmol
(cheel-MOL)

Serves 10

Common in restaurants as well as at home, chilmol is good on meats, mixed with rice, in a tortilla, or a dip for tortilla chips.

Chop well and mix together:
10 tomatoes
3–4 onions
1 clove garlic
4 sweet bell peppers
3 mint leaves
juice of 1–2 lemons (or vinegar)
salt to taste

—Yolanda Calderón de Herrera
Tegucigalpa, Honduras

Vegetable Pulau
Nepal

Serves 6

Soak **2 c. rice** in water for 2 hours. In heavy saucepan, heat for 1 minute:
1 T. oil
1 whole black cardamom
½ t. chili powder
½ t. ground cumin
Add and sauté, stirring frequently until golden:
1 med. size onion, chopped
1" piece fresh ginger root, chopped
Set aside spices and onions and add the drained rice to the oil that remains in pan. Toast until lightly browned. Add and cook slowly for about 20 minutes:
4 c. water
When rice is nearly soft, add:
1–2 c. fresh or frozen peas
½ t. salt
Serve warm with chicken or meat curry.

—Esther Lenhert
Kathmandu, Nepal

Mole de Plátano
United States / Hispanic

(MOH-lay
day
PLAH-tah-no)

Toast the following together:
  ½ oz. sesame seed
  1 stick cinnamon or 1 t. ground cinnamon
  3 whole cloves or ⅛ t. ground cloves
  3 slices bread
Put in blender and blend with:
  2 cooked tomatoes
Fry this mixture with a little vegetable oil. Add water so that the sauce is not too thick. Add:
  sugar to taste
  1 oz. melted chocolate
Peel, slice and fry in oil:
  4 ripe plantain (cooking bananas)
Add cooked bananas to chocolate mixture and boil two or three minutes. Serve.

—*Maria Arias*
Ontario, CA

Cabbage with Peanut Butter
Zimbabwe

Serves 6

In most African countries, the staple food is thick porridge made from corn meal. It is always served with relish made from a variety of fresh or dried vegetable leaves. Mushrooms, beans, meat, and sour milk also are used for relishes.

Simmer for 5–10 minutes only:
  ½ medium head of cabbage, chopped
  ½ c. water
  ½ t. salt
Add by the tablespoon, mixing well after each addition:
  1 c. peanut butter
Allow to simmer a few minutes. Serve with thick corn meal porridge.

—*Ardis Thuma*
Bradford, Ohio

Cabbage-Peanut Relish
Zambia

Serves 4

Any meat and/or vegetable dish served with insima (cornmeal porridge) in Zambia may be called a "relish." Leftover peanut relish may be added to 1–2 cups milk and used as peanut butter soup for lunch the next day.

In a skillet, heat:
2 T. cooking oil
Stir-fry, adding one vegetable at a time:
½ c. onion, sliced
3 c. cabbage, chopped
¾–1 c. tomato, diced
Add and warm thoroughly:
½–1 t. salt
a few shakes of pepper
¼ c. peanut butter

Variations: Use less cooking oil. Increase the amount of peanut butter to taste. Add **1 green pepper**, diced, with other vegetables. Add **1 c. milk** to make a sauce.

—*Kathy Stuebing; Ndola, Zambia*
Moono Anitah Cha Ii; Choma, Zambia
Anna Graybill; Hershey, PA (Zambia)
Ardys Thuma; Bradford, OH (Zambia)

Baked Cabbage
Russia

Serves 4–6

Cut into eight wedges:
1 cabbage (2–3 lbs.)
Boil 5 minutes in salted water. Take up, drain, and dry on towel. Arrange cabbage pieces neatly in a flat baking dish. Sauté in a saucepan:
1 onion, chopped
3 T. butter (or substitute)
Add:
½ c. dry bread crumbs
Brown lightly, then add:
3 T. minced parsley
salt and pepper to taste
Pour over the cabbage:
½ c. consommé or thin gravy
On top, sprinkle the browned bread crumbs and onion. Bake 30 minutes in a medium oven.

Sweet and Sour Red Cabbage
Germany

Serves 10–12

Shred into a large, deep pan:
> **2 medium-sized heads of red cabbage**
> **2 tart apples**

Add:
> **5 whole cloves**
> **1½ t. salt**
> **½ c. white wine vinegar**
> **4 c. boiling water**

Bring to a gentle boil and simmer, uncovered, for 1½ hours, stirring occasionally. Then add:
> **¼ c. butter**
> **2 T. sugar**

Simmer 30 minutes longer.

Sauerkraut
United States / Pennsylvania Dutch

Makes 3 quarts

Combine:
> **1 large head of cabbage, shredded**
> **2 T. salt**

Let stand for 1 hour. Stamp or squeeze cabbage with hands until brine appears. Pack into quart jars, being sure there is brine on the top. Do NOT turn lids tight. Let stand (somewhere out of smelling distance) for 3–4 days. As cabbage "works," some of the juice may run out. Fill up jars with boiling water (if necessary) and seal.

—Millie Sollenberger
Hagerstown, MD

Cabbage Curry
India

Gobi Torkarj
(Goh-bee TOHR-kah-ree)

Serves 6

Shred coarsely:
> **2 lbs. firm white cabbage**

Heat and sauté until golden brown:
> **1½ T. butter**
> **1 small onion, thinly sliced**

Add to above:
> **1 t. salt**
> **½ t. black pepper**
> **1 t. turmeric**

Add cabbage and mix well. Cook uncovered over medium heat until cabbage shrinks enough to cover with lid (about 15 minutes). Add:
> **1 t. lemon juice**

Cover and cook until excess liquid is absorbed (about 1 hour). Uncover and add:
> **1 T. vegetable oil**

Fry until thoroughly dry. Add and continue cooking for another 5 minutes:
> **2 t. curry powder**

Serve as a main dish for a vegetarian meal or as a side dish with a meat curry and hot, fluffy rice.

—*Ken Hoke*
Carlisle, PA (Bihar, India)

Unexpected Opportunity

There's good fishing in troubled water.

—*Spanish proverb*

Pottery vendors in Marrakech, Morocco. Photo © Corbis.

Fresh Greens with Peanut Butter
Zambia

Lupusi
(Loo-poo-see)

Zimbabwe
Isitshebo
(Eh-say-CHAY-boh)

Serves 6

Cook for 20 minutes or until soft:
  10 oz. fresh or frozen greens (chard, spinach, kale, etc.)
  1 small tomato, chopped
  1 c. water
  ¼ t. salt
Add by the tablespoon, mixing well after each addition:
  ½ c. peanut butter
Allow to simmer a few minutes. Serve with thick corn meal porridge.

—Mrs. Sharoty Hansumo Chiswakama
Mwanambia, Zambia
Abbie Dube
Bulawayo, Zimbabwe

Cauliflower and Potato Curry
India

Alu Gobi ki Subzi
(AH-loo goh-bee kee SUB-zee)

Serves 6

Sauté in **2 T. hot vegetable oil:**
2 t. ground coriander
¼ t. chili powder
¼ t. turmeric
Add and sauté for a minute or two:
1 T. green pepper, finely chopped
1 medium onion, finely chopped
Mix in:
1 medium cauliflower cut in 1-inch pieces
3 potatoes, quartered
1 t. salt
⅛ t. black pepper
Add just enough water to cook vegetables. Cover and cook until water has evaporated. Sprinkle with **1 T. lemon juice** and serve with rice or chapatis.

—*Gulabi McCarty*
Ridgeway, ON (Delhi, India)

Cabbage and Pea Curry
India

Mattar Gobi
(MAH-ter goh-bee)

Serves 6

Heat in a heavy skillet:
3 T. vegetable oil
Add and sauté:
1 medium onion thinly sliced or chopped
2 t. cumin powder
½ t. turmeric
Add and stir until coated:
½ head of cabbage, thinly sliced
½ c. water (enough to cook thoroughly)
1 t. salt
pinch of black pepper
Add, after about 20 minutes slow cooking:
½ cup tomato or V8® juice
10 oz. frozen peas
Cook about 10 minutes longer. Serve as vegetable with rice.

—*Gulabi McCarty*
Ridgeway, ON (Delhi, India)

Fried Cauliflower
Egypt

Arnabeet
(Arnah-BEET)

Serves 6–8

Cut **1 head of cauliflower** into flowerets and steam (or microwave) until tender. Don't overcook; it should retain its shape. Drain. Then beat with a fork:
> **2 eggs**

Add:
> **1 t. salt**
> **3 t. cumin**
> **6 cloves garlic, mashed (put in small plastic bag and roll with rolling pin or use garlic press)**
> **2 T. flour**

If too thick add water so it is runny but thicker than gravy. Dip each floweret into mixture and fry in deep oil until golden in color.

—Amal
Egypt

Cauliflower Soufflé
Denmark

Blomskalsgratin
(blum-skall-GRAT-in)

Serves 4

Trim and rinse **1 head of cauliflower** and cook in boiling salt water for 5 minutes. Drain and cut into flowerets. Melt in a saucepan over low heat:
> **2½ T. butter**

Add:
> **3½ T. plain flour**

Stir and gradually add:
> **1½ c. boiling milk**

Stir continually until all the milk has been absorbed. Cook 2–3 minutes. Remove saucepan from heat, season with salt and pepper and let cool. Stir one at a time into the cooked mixture:
> **4 large egg yolks**

Then add the cooked cauliflower. Whisk together until stiff:
> **4 large egg whites**
> **½ t. baking powder**

Carefully fold the egg whites into the cooked cauliflower mixture, pour into a well-greased soufflé dish, then bake for 45–60 minutes in a hot oven (400° to 425° F.). Serve hot with melted butter or tomato sauce.

Egg and Spinach Stir-Fry
China

Serves 3–4

Spinach and other vegetables are abundant and cheap at the open-air markets in China. This dish is typical of everyday fare.

Heat in large skillet or wok:

2 T. oil (peanut or soybean preferred but may use any cooking oil)

Add and sauté lightly:

2 cloves garlic, crushed or chopped fine
1 medium onion, chopped

When onions begin to soften, add and stir constantly (as if for scrambled eggs):

5 eggs, beaten

When eggs are cooked, remove mixture from wok. Rinse the wok, dry well, and again add and heat:

2 T. oil

To hot oil, add and stir constantly:

1 lb. fresh spinach, torn into small pieces

The spinach leaves will make a little liquid as you stir-fry them, or you might add a little water. When the spinach gets limp, add the egg-and-onion mixture with:

½–1 t. salt
½–1 t. soy sauce (optional)
¼–½ t. sesame oil (optional)

Serve over steamed or fried rice. Mixture is flavorful, but you may want to have soy sauce available to enhance the flavor.

—Joyce Peterman
Lancaster, PA

Crisp, Stir-Fried Kale
Brazil

Couve
(KOO-vey)

Serves 6

Cut hard stems out of:

1 lb. kale (or collard greens or Savory cabbage)

Lay flat leaves on top of each other and roll into a tight wad. Using a broad-bladed knife, cut across the roll to make shreds no more than ¼" wide. Heat in large frying pan or a wok:

2 T. sunflower oil

Stir-fry the shredded leaves rapidly until tender but still chewy. They should keep their bright green color. Season with **salt and pepper** to taste.

Collard Greens
Brazil

Serves 4–6

Collard greens are a staple food of the households of Brazil and are faithfully served on Saturdays.

Wash thoroughly and cut into shoestring-like strips:
1 bunch collard greens
In a saucepan, heat in **2 T. cooking oil** until soft. Add:
6 slices bacon, fried dry and crumbled
2 hard-boiled eggs, diced
3–4 slices fresh pineapple, minced
1 orange, peeled, sliced, and minced

—Dondeena Caldwell

Fried Green Peppers
Argentina

Chiles Fritos (chi-lays FREE-tohs)

Serves 8–10

Cut in half lengthwise:
8 green peppers
Scoop out the seeds and seed fibers. Sift together in a bowl:
¾ c. flour
1 t. baking powder
¼ t. salt
Beat in a separate bowl:
1 egg
½ c. milk
Add this to the flour mixture, stirring until smooth. Dip the peppers into the batter. Heat fat in a deep fryer to 365° F. and fry peppers in it until they are tender and browned.

Fried Zucchini Slices
France

Les Courgettes Frites
(lay kur-GETS FREE-tes)

Serves 4

Rinse well, wipe dry, and trim ends off of:
> **4 fresh, medium-size zucchini**

Slice lengthwise in ⅛" slices. Sprinkle on both sides with:
> **1 T. salt**

Allow them to sit for 15 minutes, then rinse in ice water and drain well on paper towel. Dip slices quickly in:
> **1 c. milk**

Then dredge them carefully in:
> **1 c. flour**

Make sure the slices are completely covered with the flour. Lay the floured slices on waxed paper and refrigerate for 15–30 minutes; this helps flour to adhere. Heat a large frying pan over medium heat. Add:
> **¼ c. vegetable oil**

When the oil hazes, fry the floured slices, allowing them to brown nicely on each side. Drain on paper towels and serve them very hot.

Some French chefs prefer to sprinkle fried zucchini with grated Parmesan cheese and a light dusting of dried thyme leaves before serving.

Tomato Sauce
India

Serves 6

Sauté lightly:
> **½ medium onion, chopped**
> **½ T. salad oil**

Add:
> **3–4 large tomatoes, peeled and quartered**

When tomatoes are soft, add:
> **3 T. sugar**
> **¼ t. salt**

Serve warm with rice or pasta.

—Saroj Murmu
Madhipura, Bihar

Sweet Potato Cakes
Zimbabwe

Serves 6

Cook and mash:
  1 large sweet potato
Add and mix thoroughly:
  1 egg
  1 T. sugar
  ½ c. flour
  1 T. melted margarine
  ¼ t. salt
  1 t. lemon juice and rind (optional)
  ¼ c. milk, if needed
Heat **2 T. vegetable oil** in skillet and fry the potato cakes until nicely browned on both sides.

—Jeste Mlilo
Bulawayo, Zimbabwe

Cooked Dried Corn
United States / Pennsylvania Dutch

Serves 6

Soak for 1 hour in warm water to cover:
  2 c. dried sweet corn
Cook corn until soft and the water is almost absorbed.
Stir in and bring to a boil:
  1 t. salt
  2 t. sugar
  ½ c. cream or sweet milk

—Arlene Martin
Elizabethtown, PA

Creamed Potatoes
Colombia

Papas Chorriadas
(PAH-pahs
chor-ee-AH-dahs)

Serves 4-6

In a large saucepan, cook together:
1 T. oil
1 large onion, chopped fine
4–5 medium tomatoes, peeled and chopped
Add:
1 c. water
1 t. salt
dash pepper
1 T. margarine
2 lb. medium potatoes, peeled and quartered
Cook until the potatoes are soft but not mushy. In a jar with lid, shake until smooth:
½ c. flour
1 c. milk
Pour into the tomato-potato mixture, stirring and cooking until thickened. Pour into serving dish and top with grated cheese. Serve with rice and meat.

—*Gloria de Silva*
Bogota, Colombia

Potato Casserole
Argentina

Capriotada de Papas
(kop-ree-oh-TAH-dah
day PAH-pas)

Serves 4-6

Sauté in **4 T. butter** until brown:
2 lbs. potatoes, peeled and sliced thin
1½ c. sliced onions
Sprinkle with:
2 t. salt
½ t. pepper
Cut **4 slices buttered toast** in narrow strips and arrange on bottom of buttered casserole dish. Spread some sautéed vegetables over them and moisten with:
½ c. tomato juice
Repeat for two more layers. Sprinkle top with:
½ c. grated Parmesan cheese
2 T. dry bread crumbs
Bake in 350° F. oven for 25 minutes or until browned.

Fried Potato Croquettes a la Buenos Aires
Argentina

Makes about 12

Place in a large mixing bowl:
    1½ c. mashed potatoes
Stir in:
    1 c. sifted flour
    1 c. sour cream
    2 eggs, beaten
    ½ t. baking soda
    ½ t. pepper
Melt in a skillet:
    4 T. butter
Drop the potato mixture into it by heaping tablespoons. Fry until brown on both sides. Place on paper towel and sprinkle with:
    ¼ c. minced parsley
    ½ c. stuffed green olives, chopped

Swedish Baked Potatoes
Sweden

Hasselback-potatis
(HOSS-el-bock-po-TAH-tis)

Serves 4

Peel **8 medium potatoes** and cut into thin slices three-quarters of the way through, leaving a thin uncut base so that they appear to be in a fan shape: Melt in ovenproof dish:
    ¾ T. butter
Place the potatoes in it. Sprinkle with:
    1½ t. salt
Dot with:
    ¾ T. butter
Bake in 350° F. oven for about one hour, depending on size of potatoes. After the first 30 minutes, sprinkle with grated cheese and bread crumbs.

Crispy French Fried Potatoes
France

Les Pommes Frites
(lay POM free)

Serves 4

Peel and slice:

4 large white potatoes

Cut the slices into long strips ¼" wide, washed and then well-dried with paper towels. Dredge strips well in:

1 c. flour

Make sure they are coated completely. Lay out, careful to separate each from the others, on paper towels. Heat in deep pan:

1 c. vegetable oil

Test the oil with a tiny bit of potato, which should bubble when tossed into the oil. Then add the potato strips to oil a handful at a time. Allow to just cook through, then remove with a skimmer before they begin to brown. Drain on paper towels.

Seven minutes before serving, reheat oil and fry the strips again until they are golden brown and very crisp. (This twice-fried process gives the potatoes their crispy texture.) Drain briefly on paper towels. Salt to taste and serve as soon as possible.

Corn Pie
United States / Pennsylvania Dutch

Serves 6

Line a 9" pie plate with:

½ of 2-crust pie dough

Fill with:

2 c. fresh corn cut from cob
½ c. milk
1 T. butter
2 t. salt
1 t. sugar
1 hard-boiled egg

Arrange hard-boiled egg slices over top. Cover with top crust. Pierce with fork. Bake at 325° F. for 25 minutes or longer. Serve hot with main course.

—Dorothy Ebersole
Cleona, PA

Shoe Peg Corn Casserole
United States / Southern

Serves 10

Combine:
  15-oz. can French-cut green beans
  8-oz. container sour cream (nonfat may be used)
  10¾-oz. can cream of celery soup
  ½ c. diced Velveeta cheese
  ¼ c. onion, chopped
  ¼ c. bell pepper, chopped
  2 11-oz. cans shoe peg corn
Place in 9"x13" ungreased casserole.
Mix together and top with:
  1½ c. crushed Ritz® crackers
  4 T. melted margarine
Bake at 325° F. for 45 minutes.

—*Pat Rubley*
McMinnville, TN

Eggplant in Tomato Sauce
Egypt

Betengan
(BEH-ten-gun)

Fry **1 sliced eggplant** in **1–2 T. butter or oil**. Salt to taste. Sauté in saucepan:
  1 T. minced garlic
  2 T. vegetable oil
Add:
  3 medium tomatoes, chopped
Simmer 5 minutes. Add fried eggplant and simmer for 2–3 minutes. Serve with pita bread.

—*Brian and Marcelle Zook*
Egypt

Eggplant Caviar
Russia

Baklazhannaya Ikra
(back-la-ZAHN-ya IK-ra)

Serves 4

Bake in a 350° F. oven for approximately 30 minutes:
  3 medium eggplants
Peel under cold water and discard peelings. Chop. Sauté until light brown:
  2 medium onions, minced
  2½ T. vegetable oil
Add:
  1 T. tomato paste
Stir and cook 2–3 minutes. Remove from heat and add the baked eggplant with:
  3–4 cloves garlic, mashed
  salt to taste
  cayenne pepper to taste
Serve with parsley and chopped scallions.

Vegetable Pancake
Japan

Okonomiyaki
(oh-koh-no-mee-YAH-kee)

Combine for batter:
  1 c. flour
  1 egg plus water (to make 1 c. liquid)
  ¼ t. salt
  dash monosodium glutamate (optional)
Prepare a combination of **chopped vegetables** (such as onions, carrots, green peppers, cabbage, mushrooms, and bean sprouts) for a total of approximately 3 cups. Sauté **¼ lb. any meat** (such as sausage, hamburger, squid, etc.). Mix all together and fry in pan like a pancake, using **1–2 T. vegetable oil**. Pancakes may be topped with dried fish flakes or seaweed flakes. Serve with a sprinkling of soy sauce.

—*Elaine Wright*
Okinawa, Japan

Eggplant from a French Aunt
France

Les Aubergines a la Tante
(lay so-ber-JEANS ah lah TAHN-tay)

Serves 4

Stem and peel:

2 medium-size eggplants

Cut lengthwise into ¼" slices, sprinkle on both sides with salt, then put in colander to sit and drain for 20 minutes. Rinse slices well under cold running water. Squeeze out gently and pat dry with paper towels. Dredge the slices well in:

1 c. flour

Dust off the excess. Place a large frying pan over medium heat and add:

¼ c. vegetable oil

When oil hazes, fry slices quickly until golden brown on both sides. Drain well, pressing between paper towels. Arrange slices on large platter and cover with generous sprinkling of:

½ c. freshly grated Gruyere cheese

Add a layer of:

2 medium-size, firm tomatoes, cut in paper-thin slices

Then sprinkle the tomatoes with:

1 T. virgin olive oil

1 t. pepper

¼ t. thyme leaves

¼ t. crumbled oregano

Arrange **12–16 basil leaves** over tomatoes and serve.

Contentment Is...

Belly full, heart happy.

—*Spanish proverb*

Sweet Red Beets and Eggs
United States / Pennsylvania Dutch

Wash but do not peel.

5 lbs. fresh beets

Leave ½ to 1 inch of the tops on each, so the juice does not bleed. Cover with water and boil until tender. Drain, reserving 1 c. beet liquid. Peel beets, leave whole or slice. Heat the following in a kettle until the sugar is dissolved:

1 c. beet liquid
2 c. water
1 c. sugar
1 c. cider vinegar
3 t. salt
1½ t. pepper

Add beets. Bring to a boil and boil 2 minutes. Pack in jars and seal. Marinate 6 hardboiled eggs (peeled) in the beet juice for 24 hours. If the eggs are dropped into the juice while hot, they will absorb the color and flavor better.

When serving, place small whole beets on your serving dish. Cut some eggs in half. Makes a colorful dish.

—Mary Mylin
Willow Street, PA

Squash Puppies
United States / Southern

Mix together:

1½ c. self-rising* cornmeal
½ c. self-rising* flour
½ t. baking soda

Drain and mash in a separate bowl:

1 c. tender yellow squash, cooked

Mix with:

1 egg, beaten
3 T. onions, chopped (optional)
1 c. buttermilk

Add this to dry ingredients. Drop from teaspoon into hot oil and fry. Cook until golden brown. Remove from fat and drain on absorbent paper towel. Serve hot with fish or whatever you wish.

Note: If using regular cornmeal and flour, add 2 t. baking powder.

—Tammie Burger
Smithville, TN

Squash Dressing
Southern United States

Serves 4–6

Cook and drain:
2 c. yellow squash
Add:
2 c. cornbread crumbs
1 onion, chopped
½ stick butter or margarine
**1 can condensed cream of mushroom soup
(lowfat may be used)**
1 t. sugar
1 t. sage
Mix well, then add:
1 egg, beaten
Mix thoroughly. Pour into baking dish and bake at 350°
for 30 minutes.

*—Tammie Burger
Smithville, TN*

Squash and Corn
Argentina

Calabaza con Maíz
(kah-lah-BAH-zah
kohn mah-EES)

Serves 4–6

Peel and cube:
3 lbs. yellow squash
Combine in saucepan with:
1 t. salt
Cover and cook over low heat for 30 minutes or until
soft. Watch carefully to prevent burning, and add a little
water if necessary. Sauté in a skillet for 5 minutes:
½ c. chopped onions
4 T. butter
Stir in:
1½ c. fresh or canned corn
2 t. paprika
Cook over low heat for 5 minutes. Add squash; cook
over low heat for another 5 minutes, beating in:
2 eggs
¼ c. grated Parmesan cheese

Cranberry Beans With Squash and Corn
Argentina

Porotos Granados
(por-OH-tohs
gran-AH-dohs)

Serves 6

Rinse under cold, running water:

3 c. shelled fresh cranberry beans

Combine with 5 c. water in a 5-qt. pot. Bring to boil, reduce heat to low, and let beans simmer, half-covered. In heavy 8"–10" skillet over moderate heat, combine:

¼ c. olive oil
1½ c. coarsely chopped onions
½ t. finely chopped garlic

Cook, stirring occasionally, for 5 minutes or until the onions are soft and transparent but not brown. Stir in:

6 medium tomatoes, peeled, seeded, chopped
1½ t. dried basil
1 t. dried oregano
1 lb. winter squash, seeded and cut into 1" cubes

Add a few grindings of fresh pepper, raise the heat and boil briskly, stirring, until the mixture becomes a thick puree. Add the puree to the simmering beans. Cover and cook over low heat for 1½–2 hours. When beans are tender, stir in:

½ c. fresh corn kernels or ½ c. frozen corn

Simmer 5 minutes. Season with salt and transfer the beans to a serving bowl. Serve hot in soup plates. (Note: If fresh cranberry beans are unavailable, substitute 1½ c. of dried cranberry or navy beans. Rinse them, bring to boil in 6 c. water, boil for 2 minutes. Turn off heat and let beans soak for an hour. Add the puree and squash and proceed with the recipe.)

Wedding Gifts

When a Zambian couple gets married, the boy's family is responsible for the wedding arrangements and the food, in addition to the *Labola* or bride price. The wedding is held at the boy's village and often the girl's parents do not attend. The family of the groom will send the hind leg of a cow to the parents of the bride if they do not come, so they can have a part of the celebration. When a couple decides to get married, the families decide on a *Labola*. Among other things, this includes animals, mainly cows.

—Ann Marie Parry
Danville, PA (Choma, Zambia)

Fried Plantains
Venezuela

Plátanos fritos
(PLAH-tah-nohs
FREE-tohs)

Use ripe **plantains** (cooking bananas) found in the fresh produce section of the supermarket. (They look longer and thicker than bananas.) Cut off the peel, slice lengthwise, and fry in a small amount of vegetable oil until nicely browned on both sides.

—*Thata Book*
Manheim, PA (Cagua, Venezuela)

Potato and Yogurt Curry
Nepal

Serves 8

Cut into ¼" cubes:
6 raw potatoes
Add:
¼ c. water
Cook slowly just until soft and almost dry. In a skillet, sauté until golden brown:
1 medium onion, chopped
2 T. vegetable oil
Add to above and fry for 2 minutes:
½ t. chili powder
½ t. ground cumin
½ t. turmeric
½ t. salt
Add hot potatoes and mix lightly. Fold in:
1 c. plain yogurt
Cover and heat through. Serve when hot with rice or flat bread (*chappati*).

—*Esther Lenhert*
Kathmandu, Nepal

Creamed Spinach
Russia

Sous iz shpinata
(SOOZ
ish-pee-NAH-ta)

Serves 6–8

Select, trim, and remove all stems from:

4–5 lbs. spinach (before trimming)

Wash leaves in several changes of cold water to remove all dirt, and then plunge them into a large quantity of salted, boiling water with **1 t. baking soda**. Boil until tender, drain in a fine sieve, transfer to a stoneware pot, and add:

1–2 t. sugar

Cream together thoroughly in a saucepan:

1 T. butter
1 t. flour

Then add:

1 c. cream

Heat cream mixture until hot, but not boiling. Mix with spinach. Serve with sippets, poached eggs, chopped hard-boiled eggs, omelets, fried liver, smoked ham, or fried brains.

Stuffed Baked White Turnips
Russia

Serves 6

This luncheon dish is often served with a light cream sauce.

Peel:

6 small white turnips

Bring them to a boil twice in salted water. Cook 10 minutes longer, then take them up and drain. Scoop the middle out of each turnip, leaving a thick wall. In a saucepan, cook:

1 c. Cream of Wheat® cereal (cooked in milk
according to package directions)

Allow to cool and become quite thick. Mince the scooped-out part of the turnips very fine and mix it with the Cream of Wheat®, together with:

1 egg, slightly beaten
1 T. grated cheese
salt and pepper to taste
1 T. butter

Fill the turnip shells with this mixture, piling it dome-shaped on top. Place the turnips in a baking dish. Sprinkle with **dry bread crumbs** and **1 T. melted butter**. Bake 40 minutes in a slow oven. The turnips should be nicely browned.

Baked Tomatoes
Argentina

Tomates Asados
(toh-MAH-tez
ah-SAH-dohs)

Serves 6–12

Select **6 firm, even-sized tomatoes.** Cut in half cross-wise. Mix together:
½ c. corn meal
2 T. flour
1 t. salt
¼ t. black pepper
3 T. grated onions
Brush tomatoes with:
3 T. olive oil
Then spread the corn-meal mixture on the cut side of each tomato half. Arrange in a greased baking dish; bake at 425° F. for 20 minutes or until browned and tender.

Baked Onions in Tomato Sauce
Argentina

Cebollan en Salsa de Tomate
(say-BOH-yan een
SAHL-sah day
toh-MAH-tay)

Serves 6–8

Heat in skillet:
3 T. olive oil
Sauté for 10 minutes, stirring frequently:
1 c. chopped green peppers
1½ lbs. small white onions
Add:
3 c. canned tomato sauce
1½ t. salt
¼ t. ground coriander
½ t. pepper
Pour into deep casserole dish. Cover and bake at 350° F. for 50 minutes.

Glazed Onions
Norway

Glasert Smalok
(GLASS-ert smay-LOK)

Serves 6

Pour boiling water over:
1½ lbs. small pearl onions
Then strain and peel them. Melt in a frying pan:
2 T. sugar
When it begins to turn brown, add:
1 T. butter
Stir in the onions and cook them in the caramel mixture over low-to-medium heat until evenly brown. Add enough vegetable stock or water to cover the onions and cook until tender (10–15 minutes). Do not overcook; otherwise they will not retain their shape. Serve with roast beef or any other roast meat. (*Note*: Small carrots may be glazed and served this same way.)

Green Peas with Cream
Russia

Gorokh zelenyj so slivkami
(gorok ze-LEN-ij so sliv-KAM-i)

Serves 6–8

Shell*:
2–5 lbs. fresh peas
Boil until tender and pour off water. Combine in a saucepan:
1–1½ c. cream
3 egg yolks or ½ T. flour and 1 t. butter
(creamed together)
Heat and stir until thick and very hot, but do not let it boil. Pour this sauce over the peas and serve.

(**Note*: If you prefer to serve peas in the pods, remove strings from half of peas; shell the remainder. Cut each pod in half, barely cover with water, add salt and sugar. Then proceed with the boiling stage of the recipe.)

Smothered Green Peas
France

Les Petites Pois á la Francaise
(luh pe-TEET PWA a la fran-SEZ)

Serves 4

Heat slowly in heavy stew pan over low heat:
3 T. butter
Add:
2 cups shelled young green peas
12-15 pearl onions
1 small head lettuce, chopped
Toss these vegetables in the butter until they are well coated. Use a shallow soup plate as a cover, filling the plate half full of water. Smother peas, onions, and lettuce on low heat for 50 minutes, replenishing water in soup plate if necessary. Test peas for tenderness, and when they have reached the desired degree of doneness, remove from heat and add:
1 t. sugar
1 t. chopped mint leaves
salt and pepper to taste
Toss and serve.

Stewed Green Papaya
Brazil

Refogadinho de Mamao Verde
(ree-fog-a-DEEN-oh day ma-MAH-oh VER-day)

Serves 4

Mamao is a larger version of the common papaya with a brilliant orange flesh when ripe. While still green, it can be gently stewed, which is what refogadinho *means.*

Peel skin from:
2 green papayas
Cut in half and remove large black seeds from center. Prick the flesh with fork and leave to soak in bowl of water for 1 hour to remove some of the astringency in the flavor. Drain and reserve. In frying pan, sauté in a little vegetable oil:
1 onion, chopped
When it is soft and turning golden, add:
2 garlic cloves, crushed
Cook for another minute. Stir in:
2 t. tomato paste
salt and pepper to taste
Cut papaya into 1" pieces. Stir into the mixture in the frying pan, cover, simmer for 5 minutes. Serve as an accompaniment to meat or chicken.

Sautéed Carrots
Italy

Serves 4

In a large skillet over medium heat, melt **1 T. butter or margarine**. Add:
- **3 c. thinly sliced carrots**
- **1 clove garlic, finely chopped**

Cook and stir for 5 minutes. Add:
- **½ c. chicken broth**
- **¼ t. dried marjoram leaves**
- **¼ t. dried basil leaves**

Cook uncovered until carrots are tender-crisp, about 5–7 minutes, stirring often.

Broccoli Frittata
Italy

(free-TAH-tah)

Serves 4

Heat in large, non-stick skillet:
- **2 t. olive oil**

Add:
- **2 T. minced onion**
- **1 small clove garlic, minced**

Cook 2 minutes. Add:
- **10 oz. frozen chopped broccoli, thawed**

Cook and stir until most moisture evaporates. Stir in:
- **¼ t. ground nutmeg**

In a bowl, beat together:
- **4 eggs**
- **salt and pepper to taste**

Pour this mixture over broccoli. Cover and cook over low heat 10–12 minutes without disturbing, until eggs are set. Sprinkle with:
- **½ c. shredded light mozzarella cheese**

Cook covered for 2–3 minutes more until cheese melts. Let stand 2 minutes before cutting into wedges and serving from skillet.

Homemade Pasta Sauce
Italy

Makes 11 cups

Put into a blender:

8 medium to large tomatoes, peeled and
    quartered, or 2 16-oz. cans of tomatoes
1 medium onion, quartered
¼ green pepper, cut in pieces
4 sprigs parsley
1 T. salt
3 T. cornstarch
1 clove garlic
 2 T. sugar
1 T. Italian seasoning

Process until fairly smooth. Pour into 5-qt. Dutch oven. Add:

3 6-oz. cans tomato paste
2 15-oz. cans tomato sauce
2 cups water

Bring to boil, then reduce heat and simmer 15 minutes. Package and freeze in boilable bags or freezer containers with tight fitting lids. Serve on your choice of cooked pasta.

Enjoying Italian pizza at a sidewalk cafe in Rome. Photo © Jack Hollingsworth/Corbis.

Vegetable Market Capellini
Italy

Capellini alla Mercato

(kappel-EE-nee allah mer-CAH-to)

Serves 6–8

In large saucepan over medium heat, cook and stir:
> 1 c. sliced mushrooms
> ¾ c. chopped onions
> 2 cloves garlic, chopped
> 3 T. olive oil

When the vegetables are tender, add:
> 52-oz. jar pasta sauce
> 1½ t. dried Italian seasoning

Simmer covered for 15 minutes. Then add:
> 6 oz. artichoke hearts, marinated in olive oil (drained and chopped)
> 1½ c. fresh, small cauliflower floweretes
> 1½ c. fresh, small broccoli flowerets
> ½ c. coarsely chopped bell pepper

Simmer covered 20 minutes longer or until vegetables are tender. Serve over **1 lb. hot cooked capellini**, topped with **Parmesan cheese**. (Note: *Capellini is pasta thinner than either spaghetti or vermicelli. If not available, spaghettini or vermicelli could be substituted.*)

Parmesan Bow Ties
Italy

Serves 4

Cook according to package directions and drain:
> 2 c. (uncooked measure) bow tie pasta

Transfer to a serving bowl. Add:
> ¼ c. zesty Italian salad dressing
> ¼ c. shredded Parmesan cheese
> 1 T. minced fresh parsley

Toss to coat the pasta, then serve.

Hospitality in Germany

Around the world, Germany has long been known for its delicious cuisine. But good food has not always been easy for Germans to obtain.

"We were so poor in Germany after World War II," Herb Klabunde recalls, "that most meals consisted of some kind of soup, made with whatever my mother had in the kitchen. I had so many soups that I wished all my teenage years for simple meat and potatoes." He smiles. "Now, here in the States, I have all the meat and potatoes I want, and I surely would like to have a bowl of that soup Mama used to make."

Ingrid Meneos Rogers lives in Florida. When World War II ended in Germany, she was only thirteen. Her memories of German hospitality and German foods are all highly colored by the war conditions. "We survived on cabbage and potatoes," she recalls. "Father raised rabbits so we would have some meat and I was heartbroken when we ate my favorite pet rabbit."

At age thirteen, Ingrid was cooking for a very large family of farmers and she quickly learned how to feed a table full of hungry workers: baked beans, pancakes, vegetables from the garden, hogs, and head cheese. Any pork product was a favorite of hers and that was a good thing. "Like they say, that big family I cooked for used all of the pig except the squeal." Today Ingrid remembers home and family as she eats her sentimental favorite, stuffed cabbage.

"Family reunions were great times for us in Germany," remembers Willi Kant. "Grandmother often made sauerkraut from scratch, using ceramic vats to age the cabbage; and we often had kraut and pork at the reunions. When her daughters asked about the recipe, grandmother would say she couldn't remember. 'I have no recipe,' she'd say. 'I just make it.'"

Herb Klabunde recalls that even in postwar Germany, his family stoutly observed two annual celebrations, Thanksgiving and Christmas. "We observed Thanksgiving on the first Sunday of October, and it was a time of thanking God for the harvest; our name for it was *Erntedankfest* and Mama created a meal out of whatever crops we harvested. Meat was scarce, but there were always the potatoes, green beans, and a hamburger dish that I loved. The hamburger meat was molded into egg-shaped balls and fried. I can still taste it today."

Beef Kofta (Meatball) Curry
India

Serves 50

Blend together the following:

6 med. onions, minced
36 cloves garlic, minced
6 T. Worcestershire sauce
¼ c. marjoram
2 T. thyme
3 T. salt
6 T. curry powder
6 beaten eggs

Add above mixture to:

6 lb. ground beef

Shape into balls of desired size and fry slowly. While these meatballs can be used for appetizers or for snacks, they can also be prepared as a curry main dish. To curry the meatballs, sauté in **6 T. oil:**

6 onions, chopped
2 T. ground ginger

Add and cook 5 minutes:

2 T. turmeric
2 T. curry powder
1 T. salt

Add and stir to coat:

24 med. potatoes, cubed

Then add and cook well for 5–10 minutes:

3 lbs. tomatoes, sliced
6 T. yogurt or lemon juice

Add meatballs and cover with:

3 qt. hot water

Simmer, stirring occasionally, until potatoes are tender.

Egg Curry
India

Hard-boil, peel, and cut in half lengthwise:
5½ doz. eggs
In **1 c. vegetable oil,** sauté until onions are golden:
16 medium onions, minced
2 T. and 2 t. marjoram
2 T. and 2 t. thyme
½ c. parsley flakes
Add and cook lightly for 2–3 minutes:
2 T. and 2 t. turmeric
⅓ c. salt
5 T. and 1 t. dried, unsweetened coconut
½ c. curry powder
Add the hard-boiled eggs and stir very carefully so as not to break the eggs. Also add:
32 large tomatoes, chopped
4 pts. plain yogurt
Cover the pan, lower heat, and allow to simmer for 10 minutes.

Cabbage and Beef Stew
Guyana

Serves 4

Dice and boil in **5 c. water** for 20 minutes:
1 lb. beef
While meat cooks, cut into bitesize pieces and set aside:
1½ lb. cabbage
In another container, place:
1 medium tomato, chopped
2 T. celery, chopped
2 T. fresh scallions, chopped
1 small onion, chopped
When meat has cooked, drain water and set aside. Heat a little oil in skillet over low heat. Add beef and chopped ingredients (not cabbage) to oil and cook for 2 minutes, stirring occasionally. Finally, add the cabbage with **1 t. salt and dash of pepper.** Cover and cook 15 minutes, stirring occasionally. You may add some of the reserved water during the cooking if needed. Serve with cooked rice for an evening meal.

—*Rita Lutchman*
Bronx, NY

Beef Curry
India

Korma
(KOHR-mah)

Serves 4

Heat **4 T. vegetable oil** and sauté until slightly browned:
> **2 large onions, finely chopped**

Add:
> **8–10 cloves of garlic, finely chopped**
> **2" fresh ginger root, finely chopped**

Mix well and simmer for a few minutes. Add:
> **1 lb. beef, cubed**

Coat the meat well with spices and onions. Cook for 10 minutes. Then add the following and fry for 10 minutes:
> **4 T. coriander powder**
> **5 whole cloves**
> **6 pepper corns**
> **3 bay leaves**
> **2 small pieces of cinnamon**
> **salt to taste**
> **3 T. plain yogurt**

Finally, add enough water to almost cover. Cook until meat is tender. Keep stirring often so it doesn't burn. Serve with rice.

—*Kalim Mohmad*
India

Going to market on a rainy day in Bombay. Photo © Corbis.

Shredded Beef
Nicaragua

Carne Desmenuzada
(CAR-nay des-me-noo-SAH-dah)

Serves 6

Boil **1 lb. stewing beef** until tender with:
> **2–3 cloves garlic cut in half**
> **½ t. salt**

Allow to cool. With your fingers, pull meat into fine shreds. Chop and fry together:
> **1 large onion**
> **1 large green pepper**
> **4 medium tomatoes**

Add:
> **shredded beef**
> **3 T. catsup**
> **vinegar, as desired**
> **salt, as desired**

Boil together about 5 minutes. Serve with rice and a salad of cabbage slaw, onion, and tomato. *Carne desmenuzada* can be prepared the day before and reheated. Offer your guests hot sauce at the table.

> —*Perla Estrada*
> *Managua, Nicaragua*

Lancashire Hot Pot
England

Serves 4

Put **2 lbs. cubed beef** in a deep casserole and season with salt and pepper to taste. Arrange the following ingredients in thin layers over the meat:
> **2 large onions, sliced**
> **1 c. carrots, sliced**
> **1½ lb. potatoes, sliced**

End with a layer of potatoes arranged in overlapping slices. Pour 1 c. beef stock over the above ingredients and cover. Put in 325° F. preheated oven. Cook for 2–2½ hours or until meat is tender. Increase temperature to 400° F., uncover, and cook for 30 minutes or until top layer of potatoes is brown.

> —*June Simmonds*
> *London, England*

Beef Tongue in Sauce
Nicaragua

Lengua en Salsa
(LEHN-gua en SAHL-sah)

Serves 10 or more

Beef tongue is prepared only for special occasions because it is expensive to make. Since it must boil so long, it uses a lot of gas or firewood.

Wash **1 beef tongue** in salt water. Place in a large pan and cover with water. Boil 2–3 hours until tongue is soft. Peel off the skin that covers the tongue and slice tongue. Then melt in large frying pan:

¼ c. margarine

Add the sliced tongue with:

⅓ c. catsup
½ t. salt
pinch of sugar
½ c. water

Cook for about 25 minutes on low heat, adding water as needed. Serve on a platter and garnish with:

½ c. chopped celery on top of tongue
½ c. cooked peas around the edges
sliced olives, if you wish
a couple of parsley sprigs in the corners

Serve with rice and a salad.

—*Martiza Mairena*
Managua, Nicaragua

Grilled Steak
France

Le Steak Frites
(luh steak FREE)

Serves 4

Heat grill or broiler. Pepper both sides of **4 thin steaks (round or rump)** and lay out flat on clean, hard surface. With meat pounder (serrated if possible) or edge of small dinner plate, pound steaks all over on both sides. With brush, apply **¼ c. vegetable oil or butter** on both sides of steaks and grill them. Time for rare to well done varies from one minute on each side to 5 minutes on first side and 4 on second. Sprinkle steaks with thyme (if you wish) and serve at once with a generous serving of Crispy French Fried Potatoes (see recipe).

Beef Stroganov
Russia

Serves 4–6

Cut **1½ lbs. sirloin tip or filet** into longish strips about ¼" thick, season with salt and pepper, and sprinkle with **1½ T. flour**. In a heavy-bottomed skillet, heat:

1 T. oil

1 T. butter (optional)

Begin browning the beef in batches—only one layer at a time in the skillet—and remove browned meat to a plate. Repeat, adding a little oil and butter as needed, until all the beef is sautéed; then add a little more oil and sauté:

1 medium onion, chopped

When the onions are golden, add:

1 c. bouillon or beef stock

1 t. Dijon or Pommery mustard

1½ T. tomato paste

Simmer until thickened; return beef to skillet and simmer for another 3–5 minutes. Remove from heat, stir in:

½ c. sour cream

Adjust seasoning to taste and sprinkle with parsley.

(*Note*: Although in the United States beef stroganov is usually served over buttered noodles, it is traditionally presented in Russia over very thick, fried potato wedges.)

Variations: Try less expensive and/or leaner cuts of beef such as rump roast or round steak. However, for these cuts you should increase the simmering time about 15 minutes or until the meat is tender. The oldest Russian recipes use less sour cream while Polish versions use more. Many people also like sliced mushrooms in their stroganov; if so, sauté them with the onions to reduce liquid. Another optional seasoning is Worcestershire sauce.

Gratin of Boiled Beef with Onion Sauce
France

Le Boeuf en Miroton
(luh bou-FAHN in mirro-TON)

Serves 4

Heat heavy frying pan and add:

2 T. vegetable oil

When it sizzles, add:

3 medium-size onions, peeled and finely ground

Reduce heat to its lowest mark. Sauté onions slowly, stirring with a wooden spatula from time to time so they cook evenly and do not burn. When onions turn a bit golden, sift over them:

1 T. flour

Stir carefully. Smooth out any lumps. Let cook for 3 minutes, stirring constantly. Add:

1½ c. beef broth or water

Stir vigorously. Then add:

1 T. wine vinegar
½ t. salt
¼ t. pepper
1 bay leaf
1 plump garlic clove, peeled

Allow to simmer for 8 minutes. Preheat oven to 400° F. Lightly oil a shallow baking dish. Discard bay leaf and garlic and put a little of the sauce in the bottom of the dish. Spread it lightly over bottom and sprinkle it evenly with:

12–16 preserved capers
2 T. coarsely chopped sour pickle

Arrange slices of beef in overlapping layers on top of capers and pickle. Cover beef with sauce, spreading the rather thick sauce evenly so it covers beef and touches edges of the baking dish. Sprinkle the sauce with an even coating of bread crumbs and dot the surface with little knobs of butter. Bake till golden and serve.

Wild horses at Los Glacieares National Park, Argentina. Photo © Corbis.

Broiled Steak with Peanut Sauce
Argentina

Cariucho
(kah-ree-oo-choh)

Serves 4–6

Heat in skillet:
> **3 T. olive oil**

Sauté in the oil for 5 minutes:
> **1 c. chopped onions**
> **½ c. chopped green peppers**

Add:
> **1 c. chopped tomatoes**
> **1½ t. salt**
> **¼ t. dried, ground chili peppers**
> **1 t. paprika**

Cook over low heat for 5 minutes. Mix in:
> **1 c. ground peanuts**
> **1½ c. chicken broth**

Simmer for 30 minutes, then stir in:
> **¼ c. heavy cream**

Adjust seasonings to taste. Broil **5 lbs. sirloin steak** to desired degree of doneness. Slice the steak and pour sauce over it. Serve with boiled potatoes.

Veal Roll
Argentina

Pecho o Aleta de Ternera
(PAY-choh oh ah-LAY-tah day ter-NER-ah)

Serves 6–9

Debone and pound as thin as possible:

1 breast of veal

Season with:

2½ t. salt
½ t. pepper
2 t. paprika

Heat in a skillet:

2 T. olive oil

Sauté for 5 minutes:

½ lb. ham, chopped

Make an omelet of:

3 eggs
1 t. salt

Sprinkle the ham on it and roll up. Place the omelet on the veal and arrange **12 sour gherkin pickles** over it. Roll up the veal breast and tie with thread. Then heat in a casserole or Dutch oven:

3 T. olive oil

Brown the meat in it on all sides. Remove and sauté until browned:

1 c. chopped onions
½ c. grated carrots

Mix in:

1 c. chopped tomatoes

Cook for 5 minutes. Return the meat and add:

1 bay leaf
3 T. minced parsley
¼ t. thyme
½ c. water

Cover and bake in 350° F. oven for 2 hours, basting occasionally and adding a little more water if necessary. Add:

1 c. sliced, stuffed olives

Bake 10 minutes longer. Slice and serve.

Calf's Liver, Berlin Style
Germany

Kalbsleber Berliner Art
(KAHLB-sleb-ber beur-LEEN-er art)

Serves 6

Melt **2 T. butter** in a heavy 12" skillet over moderate heat. Add:

2 large Spanish onions, peeled and halved, then sliced ¼" thick

Sauté the onions, stirring often, until limp and golden; transfer to large bowl and reserve. Melt another **2 T. butter** in skillet and add :

2 large Golden Delicious or Rome Beauty apples, peeled, cored, and cut into wedges

Sauté the apples about 5 minutes, stirring often, until golden; transfer to separate bowl and reserve. Prepare:

1½ lbs. calf's liver, sliced ¼" thick

Dredge the liver in:

3 T. all-purpose flour

Shake off the excess flour. Melt **2 T. butter** in skillet over high heat and, as soon as it foams up and subsides, add half the liver and brown 1–2 minutes on a side, depending on whether you like liver rare or medium-rare. Lift the browned slices to a heated platter and sprinkle each lightly with salt and pepper. Tent with foil to keep warm. Add the remaining liver to skillet and brown as before. Transfer to platter and season with salt and pepper. Pile the onions and apples on top of liver, sprinkle with **2 T. minced parsley**, and serve.

"Is That a Turkey?"

I planned to visit our son John, who was teaching at Choma Secondary School in Zambia. while there I wanted to have a party for many of our American friends. Could I carry a turkey all the way to Zambia? Into my carry-on bag went the frozen turkey, packed in dry ice!

When the bag went through the scanner in London's Heathrow Airport, the handsome young inspector asked, "Is that a turkey?"

When I admitted it was, he replied, "I've seen worse!"

—*Mary Long*
Grantham, PA

Sauerbraten
Germany

(sour-BRAH-ten)

Serves 12–14

Rinse and trim any excess fat from:
  1 beef top round roast (about 4 lbs.)
Combine in a saucer:
  2 t. salt
  1 t. ground ginger
Rub these spices over roast. Place in a deep glass bowl.
In a saucepan, combine:
  2½ c. water
  2 c. cider vinegar
  2 medium onions, sliced
  ⅓ c. sugar
  2 T. mixed pickling spice
  1 whole peppercorn
  8 whole cloves
  2 bay leaves
Bring to a boil, then pour this marinade over the roast; turn to coat. Cover and refrigerate for 2 days, turning twice a day. Remove roast from refrigerator, reserving marinade; pat roast dry. In a large kettle or Dutch oven, brown roast on all sides in **2 T. vegetable oil**. Strain marinade, reserving half of the onions and seasonings. Pour 1 cup marinade and reserved onions and seasonings over roast in a large kettle. (Cover and refrigerate the remaining marinade.) Bring to a boil. Reduce heat, cover, and let simmer for 3 hours or until meat is tender.

Gravy
Strain cooking liquid, discarding the onions and seasonings. Measure liquid; if necessary, add enough reserved marinade to equal 3 cups. Pour this into a saucepan and bring to rolling boil. Add:
  14–16 gingersnaps, crushed
Simmer until gravy is thickened. Slice roast and serve with gravy.

Roast Spareribs
Sweden

Ugnstekt Revbensspjall
(YOU-gun-stek rev-BEN-sp'jal)

Serves 6

Trim excess fat from:
3–4 lbs. spareribs
Rub the meat with:
½ t. ground white pepper
½ t. salt
¾ t. powdered ginger or dry mustard
Melt **1½ t. butter** in heavy cast-iron casserole and brown the meat on both sides. Cover meat and continue roasting in 350° F. oven for about 1½–1¾ hours until tender. Pour **1 c. boiling water** into casserole and baste meat from time to time. Finally, pour in:
1 cup prune juice
Strain the juices, skim off fat, and pour this sauce into a sauce boat. Serve with boiled potatoes, applesauce, and cooked prunes.

Pan Sautéed Meat and Vegetables
Japan

Teppanyaki
(tay-pahn-YAH-kee)

Quick-fry using a small amount of salad oil in a frying pan before your guests:
1 lb. beef, thinly sliced
2 onions, sliced
1 pack mushrooms, sliced
1 pack bean sprouts
1–2 green peppers, sliced
1 pack tofu, cubed
¼–½ cabbage, cut coarsely
Make a dipping sauce of the following ingredients:
½ c. sake (Japanese rice wine) or sherry
⅓ c. soy sauce
dash monosodium glutamate (optional)
1 t. mustard or grated fresh ginger
Dip meat and vegetables in sauce and eat with steamed rice.

—*Elaine Wright*
Okinawa, Japan

Moussaka
Greece

(moo-SA-kah)

Serves 8

Served with crusty bread and a Greek salad, moussaka is a popular Greek dish.

Peel and cut in ½" slices:
2 large or 3 small eggplants
Layer on a platter. Salt each layer lightly, if desired. Cover with plastic wrap for 45 minutes so that moisture can be drawn out. Oil a 9"x13" casserole and place prepared eggplant slices on bottom in a single layer. Bake in 450° F. oven for 8–10 minutes. Do not turn.

Meat Mixture:
Sauté in **2 t. vegetable oil**:
2 medium onions, chopped
2 garlic buds, crushed
Add to the above and brown evenly:
1½ lbs. lean ground beef
salt and pepper to taste
When browned, add and simmer gently until liquid is absorbed:
18-oz. can tomato paste
½ c. water
¼ c. grated Parmesan cheese

Sauce:
In a saucepan, melt:
6 t. butter or margarine
Add and stir until smooth:
10 T. flour
Add gradually and stir constantly until thickened:
4 c. warm milk (may use powdered milk)
Add, stirring until melted:
1½ c. grated Parmesan cheese
Remove from heat. In mixing bowl, beat:
6 eggs (or equivalent egg subtitute)
Add a little of the cooked sauce to eggs while beating on low speed of mixer. Add this to the remaining sauce in saucepan.

Remove eggplant from oven and spread the meat mixture over it. Pour sauce over eggplant-and-meat mixture. If desired, sprinkle with cinnamon or nutmeg. Bake at 350° F. for one hour. Allow to cool slightly and cut into squares.

—*Beulah Heisey*
Mechanicsburg, PA (Greece)

Meat Sauce with Egg
Egypt

Shakshouka
(shuk-SHOO-kah)

Fry together:
> **1 lb. ground beef**
> **2 onions, chopped**

Add and cook:
> **1 pepper, chopped**
> **2–3 tomatoes, chopped**
> **1 small can tomato sauce**
> **salt and pepper to taste**

Break 1 egg in mixture and cook until set (cover and simmer, or put in oven for 5 minutes). Serve with pita bread.

—Brian and Marcelle Zook
Egypt

Steak and Eggplant Stew
South Africa

Serves 6

Heat **1 T. cooking oil** in a large saucepan, add and braise lightly:
> **1 large onion, chopped**
> **1 large eggplant, chopped**
> **1 lb. stewing beef coated with 2 T. flour**

Add:
> **1 c. water**
> **1 c. uncooked rice**
> **16-oz. can crushed tomatoes**
> **1 t. salt**
> **1 beef bouillon cube**
> **¼ t. cayenne pepper**
> **½ t. parsley**
> **½ t. coriander**
> **½ t. lemon dill**
> **½ t. garlic**
> **1 t. cilantro (coriander leaf)**

Bring to a boil and simmer for 45 minutes to 1 hour, adding more water gradually as needed.

—Rosina Madlabane
Soshanguve, South Africa

Beef Shanks with Star Anise
Papua New Guinea

We met Jackson Tsang in church while he was a student in Sydney, Australia, years before we were missionaries to Madang. After our return to the United States, Jackson came to visit us for a week. He prepared our evening meals using recipes like this one.
—Roger L. Williams

Select **1 beef shank** for each person to be served. Coat the shanks with flour and sear in a pan with hot olive oil or vegetable oil until the flour has browned into a crust all around the shanks. Place the seared shanks into a large pot that will hold enough water to cover the shanks without boiling over. Add enough water to cover the shanks, followed by:

½ **c. soy sauce**
2–3 **star anise per shank**
4–6 **slices fresh ginger**
2–3 **cloves garlic**

Bring the pot to a boil, then reduce the heat and allow to simmer for 1 hour or so, until the shanks are tender. Serve with white rice.

—Jackson Tsang
Madang, Papua New Guinea

A fisherman in the clear coastal waters of Brazil. Photo © Ricardo Junqueira/Corbis.

Traditional Indian Stew
Nicaragua

Indio Viejo
(EEN-dee-oh
vee-AY-hoh)

Serves 4-6

Traditional Indian stew is eaten in many Nicaraguan homes. The consistency is thick and heavy, but the flavor is savory and the contents nourishing.

Boil until tender:
  1 lb. stewing beef
When cool, pull into threads with fingers. Save the broth. Mix with broth and enough water to make a thick mixture:
  1 c. cornmeal
Set this cornmeal paste aside. In a cooking pot, fry together:
  1 onion, chopped
  1 tomato, chopped
  3 cloves garlic, chopped
  1 green pepper, finely chopped, if desired
  shredded meat
When vegetables are soft, add the cornmeal paste and cook, stirring constantly for about 20 minutes or until the consistency is thick and it is brown in color. Add broth as needed during cooking. Finally, add:
  2 sprigs mint, chopped
  1–2 T. lemon juice
  salt to taste

—*Juana Hernández*
Managua, Nicaragua

Your Tone of Voice

Because Chinese is a tonal language, the same syllable can be pronounced with different tones and have several different meanings. Take for example the syllable *ji* (pronounced "jee"). If this syllable is pronounced using a high, flat tone, it means "chicken." If it is pronounced in a rising tone, as if asking a question ("Jee?"), it can mean "illness." If it is pronounced in a tone that falls from a high pitch to a low pitch, it can be a person's surname.

When my missions teammate and I were introduced to a young man named Mr. Ji, we remembered the syllable correctly but failed to get the right tone. You can imagine our embarrassment when, after some months of acquaintance with him, his girlfriend gently informed us that we had been calling him "Mr. Chicken"!

—*Joyce Peterman*
Manheim, PA

Meat and Macaroni
Egypt

Macarona bel Bishemal
(mak-a-ROW-nah bell-bish-eh-MALL)

Boil **1 lb. macaroni** (preferably the 1½" long type), then strain. In a skillet, sauté:

>   **1 large onion, diced**

Add and cook until brown:

>   **2 lbs. ground beef**

Add:

>   **pinch of salt and pepper**

To make the *bishemal* sauce, melt **2 T. butter** in a saucepan on low heat. Add and cook until yellow:

>   **3 T. flour**

Add a little at a time and stir constantly until thick:

>   **3 c. (or more) chicken soup**
>   **1 c. milk**

Mix the macaroni, meat, and half of the *bishemal* sauce; pour into a baking dish. Cover the mixture with the remainder of the *bishemal* and top with **2 beaten eggs**. Bake at 350° F. for 45 minutes or until brown.

>   —*Brian and Marcelle Zook*
>   *Egypt*

Chicken Pie
Québec

Paté au Poulet
(pah-tay oh poo-lay)

Serves 6

Melt in large saucepan:

>   **½ c. margarine**

Add:

>   **½ c. flour**

Slowly add, stirring constantly:

>   **3 c. chicken broth**
>   **salt and pepper to taste**

Cook on medium heat about one minute until it bubbles. Remove from heat and add:

>   **3 c. chicken or turkey, cooked and cubed**
>   **1½ c. carrots, cooked and sliced**
>   **1 c. peas, cooked (optional)**

Pour into 9"x13" pan. Cover with pastry crust. Bake at 425° F. for 20 minutes or until golden.

>   —*Yolande Shink*
>   *Romuald, Québec*

Zimbabwean Stew
Zimbabwe

Serves 4

Every Zimbabwean girl, as young as 10 years old, is able to make this stew.

Fry lightly until browned:
   1 lb. beef, cubed
Add and sauté lightly:
   2 T. oil
   2 small onions, chopped
Add and cook:
   3 ripe medium-size tomatoes, chopped
   salt and pepper to taste
When you have achieved the desired seasoning, add:
   1½ c. water
Simmer until meat is tender. Serve with rice or corn meal porridge.

Variations:
Vegetables such as carrots, green beans, peas, or potatoes may be added after the addition of liquid. Sometimes green leafy vegetables—e.g., cabbage or spinach—are added before the addition of water and fried a little. In that case, reduce the water to less than ½ cup.

—*Jeste Mlilo*
Bulawayo, Zimbabwe

Curried Meat
Zambia

Serves 4–6

Sambals are small dishes of chopped tomatoes, chopped onions, sliced bananas, chutney or apricot jam, raisins, peanuts, shredded coconut, pineapple chunks.

Fry or cook, then set aside:
   ½ lb. beef or lamb, cubed
Heat **2 T. oil or drippings** and sauté:
   1 large onion, sliced
Add and heat until it bubbles:
   1 t. curry powder
Then add:
   2–3 peeled tomatoes, chopped
   2 t. chutney
   a few raisins
   1 t. salt
   1 t. lemon juice
   1 c. water
Stir the prepared meat into the curry sauce. Cook slowly with lid on saucepan for about 1 hour or less. Serve on boiled rice with *sambals* placed on top.

—*Anna Graybill*
Hershey, PA (Zambia)

Cornbread Taco Bake
United States / Southern

Serves 6

In skillet, brown and drain:
1½ lbs. ground beef
Add:
1 package (1 oz.) Durkee® taco seasoning
½ c. water
12-oz. can whole kernel corn (drained)
½ c. green peppers, chopped
8 oz. tomato sauce
Pour the above ingredients into a 2-qt. casserole. In a separate bowl, prepare according to directions:
8½ oz. package corn muffin mix
Add:
half of 2.8-oz. can Durkee® French fried onions
Spoon muffin mix around outer edge of dish. Bake uncovered at 400° F. for 20 minutes. Top with:
⅓ c. shredded cheddar cheese
remaining fried onions
Bake 2–3 minutes longer.

—*Avelene Weber*
West Milton, OH

Tribal hunters on the savannah in Tanzania, Africa. Photo © Corbis.

Meat-Stuffed Grape Leaves
Jordan

Serves 4–8

Combine for stuffing:

1½ lb. ground lamb or beef or a mixture of both (should have some fat)
1 c. onions, chopped
1 c. canned tomatoes
¾ c. raw rice
½ c. fresh parsley, chopped or ¼ c. dry parsley flakes
salt and pepper to taste

Prepare:

8-oz. jar of grape leaves

Line a heavy pot with a layer of leaves or use a trivet to prevent the bottom layer from sticking to the pot. Separate and drape some of the leaves around the inside of the pot. Now shape a portion of stuffing into a small cylinder and place it on a leaf near the stem end, after pinching off the remaining piece of stem. Fold down the lobes near the stem, fold in the sides, and roll toward the point of the leaf. Arrange the stuffed leaves side by side in the pot, making as many layers as necessary. Pour over the stuffed leaves:

2 c. canned tomatoes
½ c. water
½ t. salt

Cover, bring to a boil, then lower heat and simmer about one hour. Test for doneness by tasting one (or more!). Serve hot. Leftovers may be frozen.

Variations:
(1) Substitute ¼ c. coarse ground bulgur wheat for the same amount of rice or ¼ c. wheat germ for part of the rice. (2) Top with plain yogurt.

—*Ethel Kreider*
Lancaster, PA (Jordan)

Chicken Curry
India

Serves 10

We often ate chicken curry and rice on a banana leaf with our fingers, served in the courtyard or on a veranda.

In **2 T. hot cooking oil**, toast:

¼ t. cumin seeds

2 black cardamom pods

1 white cardamom pod

When oil crackles, add and fry until brown:

3 large onions, chopped

1" piece of ginger root, sliced or

½ t. ginger powder

6 cloves garlic, sliced

Mix the following with **2 T. water** and fry with onion mixture for 2 minutes:

½ t. ground cumin

3 T. ground coriander

¼ t. turmeric

¼ t. cinnamon

⅛ t. cloves

¼ t. salt or to taste

¼ t. hot red chili powder or to taste

Add **2-lb. fryer chicken**, cut in 1" pieces, including bones. Brown chicken in the curry mixture, then add:

1 c. water

Add more as water is absorbed. Cover and cook slowly for 30 minutes, allowing flavors to blend. Toward end of cooking time, add:

1 large tomato, chopped

Allow to steam for 5 minutes. More water may be added for a gravy consistency. Serve with brown or white rice. Also lentils can be served as an accompaniment.

—Beulah Arnold
  Campbellsville, KY (India)
 Gulabi McCarty
  Ridgeway, ON (India)

Chicken in Mustard Sauce
Argentina

Pollo en Salsa de Mostaza
(POH-yoh een SAHL-sah day mohs-TAH-zah)

Serves 6–8

Wash and pat dry:
2 3-lb. fryers, disjointed
Season with:
2½ t. salt
½ t. pepper
Melt in a large pot:
4 T. butter

Brown the chicken in it. Add:
1 c. chicken bouillon
1 c. water
Cover and cook over low heat for 45 minutes or until tender. Beat together in the top of a double boiler:
3 eggs
3 T. lemon juice
1 ½ t. dry mustard
1 t. sugar
Cook this mixture in the double boiler, stirring steadily until thickened. Add gravy from chicken to the mixture, and pour the resulting sauce over chicken. Cook over low heat, basting often until chicken is well cooked.

Charcoal Broiled Chicken on a Skewer
Japan

Yakitori
(yah-kee-TOE-ree)

Serves 8

Cut 2 chicken breasts in 1" pieces and place on bamboo skewers. Prepare basting sauce by simmering for 15 minutes:
¾ c. *sake* (Japanese rice wine) or sherry
¾ c. soy sauce
¼ c. sugar
½ t. grated fresh ginger (optional)
Brush sauce over chicken skewers and broil over charcoal. Turn frequently, brushing more sauce over meat. Serve hot. Chicken livers are also delicious cooked in this sauce.

—*Elaine Wright*
Okinawa, Japan

Chicken Tikka
India

Murghi Tikka
(MOOR-gee TEE-kah)

Serves 8

Blend the following ingredients in blender:

¼ c. lemon juice
2 T. vinegar
¼ c. parsley
2 cloves garlic
½ t. ground ginger
1½ t. paprika
½ t. cayenne pepper
1 t. turmeric
1 t. ground cumin
1 t. salt (or to taste)
½ c. plain nonfat yogurt or tomato juice

Pour sauce over:

2 lbs. boneless, skinless chicken breast cut into small pieces

Refrigerate and marinate for 2 hours. Then add:

½ c. frozen peas
3 medium potatoes, cubed

Cook slowly for 45 minutes to 1 hour. Add water as the chicken cooks, 1–2 T. at a time, to create the curry sauce. Serve with steamed rice. Best served with lentils and a chutney of sliced onions and tomatoes.

—*Erma I. Sider*
Mechanicsburg, PA (Bihar, India)

A Deer or a Leopard?

I had left my gun with my friend, Arthur Singh, so that he could take it to the Supaul government office to renew my license. He asked for some shells to do a little hunting. The evening before he planned to return the gun, he went out into the jungle to look for wild game. Sure enough, a pair of eyes glowed in the dark. Arthur shot and killed a deer. The next day he brought a leg of venison with the gun.

Arthur returned to Supaul to find the village folk asking why he had not brought home the leopard he had shot the previous night. He told them he shot a deer, but they insisted a dead leopard was lying in the jungle. Sure enough, he found a leopard lying near where he shot the deer. The leopard probably pounced on the deer at the exact moment that Arthur shot, thus killing both animals.

—*William R. Hoke*

Chicken Biriani
India

Murghi Biriani
(MURG-ee beer-ee-YAN-ee)

Serves 8

Cut up in small pieces:
- **3 lbs. chicken**

Add to chicken and marinate for 30 minutes:
- **1 c. plain yogurt**
- **½ c. onion, chopped**
- **2 T. coriander powder**
- **½ t. fresh ginger root, grated**
- **1 t. garlic, minced**
- **1 t. turmeric**
- **¼ t. black pepper**

In a skillet, sauté together until onion turns light brown:
- **¼ c. butter, melted**
- **¼ c. vegetable oil**
- **1 medium onion, finely chopped**
- **2 cloves garlic, minced**
- **8 whole cloves**
- **8 whole cardamom**
- **1 t. salt**
- **1 c. water**

Add the marinated chiken and sauté further, stirring frequently. When chicken has changed color and sauce seems dry, add **1 c. water**, lower heat and simmer for 30 minutes. Add **1 chicken bouillon cube** with enough additional water to make 4 c. curry sauce. Remove chicken pieces from sauce and set aside. Heat this curry sauce until almost boiling. Meanwhile rinse and soak for 30–40 minutes:
- **3 c. Basmati rice or long grain rice**

Sauté in a saucepan until onion is wilted:
- **1 small onion, sliced thin**
- **4 oz. butter or oil**
- **1 clove garlic, minced**
- **4 whole cloves**
- **8 cardamom, gently crushed**
- **2 2" sticks cinnamon**

Transfer rice and this mixture to a 9"x13" baking dish and stir until rice is warmed through. Add the boiling-hot curry sauce and stir. Cover and bake at 325° F. for 30 minutes. Then place the chicken pieces in the rice, cover again, and bake for another 30 minutes. Serve with chutney and raita salad.

—*A. J. Mann*
Elizabethtown, PA (Bihar, India)

Chicken in Coconut Milk
Thailand

Heat this broth in a 2-qt. saucepan:
   2 c. water
   milk drained from 1 fresh coconut*
   ½ c. thin slices of galangal
   1 stem lemon grass, sliced into thin rings and crushed
   3 T. fish sauce
Cook in this broth until tender:
   6 chicken drumsticks
Season at end of cooking with:
   juice of 3 lemons
   3–4 kaffir lime leaves
   10 hot chilies, crushed
Put into serving dish and sprinkle with coriander leaves, chopped.

Variation:
May substitute for fresh coconut milk by mixing 2 c. water with ½ lb. grated coconut and then squeezing out milk.

—*Kathy Brubaker*
Bangkok, Thailand

Hospitality and Justice

Biblical hosts showed "love of strangers" by making sure that their guests received food, drink, clothing, shelter, and respect. When at table, however, hosts served lamb, calves' meat, bread, fruit, and wine—foods of their culture. Food, drink, clothing, shelter, and respect are basic necessities of life. Hospitality and justice are therefore linked in the Bible. When some individuals or groups lack these necessities, justice is not fully present in society.

To address lack of justice in biblical times, Israel created laws to help strangers, widows, and orphans, some of the most vulnerable people in society—people whom Jesus would have called "the least of these." For example, Exodus records this command: "You shall not wrong or oppress a resident alien, for you were aliens in the land of Egypt. You shall not abuse any widow or orphan. If you do abuse them, when they cry out to me, I will surely heed their cry" (22:21–23).

—Nancy A. Carter, "Chicken & Biscuits and More"
United Methodist General Board of Global Ministries

Chicken and Vegetables Cooked in Broth
Japan

Mizutaki
(mee-zoo-TAH-kee)

Serves 4

Cook in **5 c. water** for 30 minutes:
4 chicken thighs or breasts
Season to taste. Cut up chicken. Place in an electric fry pan at the table. Add:
4 c. of chicken broth
4 long onions or leeks, cut diagonally
8 oz. package mushrooms, shiitake or enoki
8 oz. package tofu, cubed
1 Chinese cabbage, cut coarsely
Cook until cabbage is tender. In each person's soup bowl, mix a little soy sauce and lemon juice to taste (monosodium glutonate optional). Add broth, vegetables, and chicken from frying pan. Eat with rice in separate bowl, using chopsticks, or pour over bowl of rice and eat with spoon like thick soup. Especially good served in winter.

—Ruth Zook
Mechanicsburg, PA (Japan)

Tonga Chicken
Zambia

Nkuku
(in-KOO-koo)

Serves 5

Brown in **2 T. vegetable oil**:
1 chicken, cut in pieces
Add and cook on medium heat for 30 minutes:
4 medium tomatoes, chopped
1 small onion, diced
Mix together:
1 t. curry powder
1 T. flour
1½ c. water
1 t. salt
Add to chicken mixture and cook until thickened. Serve with *nshima* (cornmeal porridge).

—Shelly Muleya, Mizinga Village,
Choma, Zambia
Arbys E. Thuma
Bradford, OH (Zambia)

Chicken Stew
Cuba

Fricasé De Polio
(free-kah-SAY day POH-yoh)

Serves 6–8

My grandmother taught me this typical Cuban dish when she taught me how to cook. We measured nothing and tasted everything.

In a large pot, sauté in **¼ c. olive oil:**
  1 whole chicken, skinned and cut up
  1 large onion, cubed
  1 green pepper, cubed
  2–3 garlic cloves, mashed
Add:
  2 bouillon cubes
  1 t. cumin
  ½ t. salt
  dash pepper
After browning, add and stir:
  4-oz. can tomato sauce
  1 t. turmeric or saffron
  3–4 potatoes, cut in chunks
  3–4 carrots, cut in chunks
  salt, if needed
  enough water to cover chicken
Simmer about 1 hour and serve over rice. Goes nicely with a garden salad. Leftovers make great chicken soup by using the deboned chicken and adding water and noodles.

—*Merly Bundy*
Madrid, Spain

Chicken Enchilada
United States / Navajo

Serves 6

Cook and remove from bones:
  2 lbs. chicken
Mix together:
  1 can cream of mushroom soup
  1 medium can enchilada sauce
Layer in a 2-qt. casserole half of each:
  chicken
  6 corn tortillas, large
  soup mixture
Repeat the above layers, then top with:
  1 lb. cheddar cheese, grated
Bake at 350° F. for 50 minutes.

—*Ethel Bundy*
Mechanicsburg, PA (New Mexico)

Chicken with Vegetables and Tofu
China

Serves 4

Tofu *(TOE-fu) is soybean curd, a good source of vegetable protein. Oriental people often use it as a meat substitute.*

Cut into ½" cubes and return to refrigerator:

10 oz. firm tofu, drained

Cut into thin strips:

1 chicken breast, skinned and boned

Marinate chicken for at least 10 minutes in:

1 T. cornstarch
1 T. soy sauce
1 clove garlic, minced

Blend:

¾ c. chicken broth
1 t. vinegar
1 T. cornstarch
2 T. soy sauce

In very hot wok or skillet, heat:

1 T. vegetable oil

Add chicken, stir-fry 2 minutes, then remove from wok. In the same wok, heat:

2 T. vegetable oil

Add and stir-fry 2 minutes:

1 medium zucchini, julienned
1 red or green bell pepper, cut into strips
¼ lb. mushrooms, quartered
1 t. fresh ginger root, minced
4 green onions, cut into 2" lengths (whites only)

Add and stir-fry 1 minute:

green onion tops

Add chicken and broth mixture and stir until thickened. Fold in tofu and heat through. Serve at noon or for the evening meal, either with rice or noodles.

—Mim Stern
Philadelphia, PA

Friends taste one another's dishes in Beijing, China. Photo © Yang Liu/Corbis.

Stir-Fry Chicken and Vegetables
Japan

Cut into bite-size pieces:
   2 chicken breasts
Marinate in:
   ¼ c. soy sauce
   2 T. mirin (sweetened rice wine or cooking sherry)
Fry chicken until just done; do not overcook. Add and cook until thickened:
   1 c. bouillon
   2 T. cornstarch
In separate fry pan, stir-fry in oil until crisp-tender:
   1 onion
   8 oz. bean sprouts
   8 oz. shiitake mushrooms
   6 oz. broccoli or sugar peas, or any seasonal vegetable
Add vegetables to meat mixture. Heat through and serve over rice or noodles (drained Ramen Noodles® make a quick meal).

—*Ruth Zook*
Mechanicsburg, PA (Japan)

Filipino Chicken
Philippines

Serves 4–6

This comes from my husband's voluntary service days in the Philippines. When I prepare this, he says it brings back the sights, sounds, and smells of Filipino villages.

In large skillet, place:
1 frying chicken cut in pieces (or two breasts cut in half)
Spoon over the chicken:
4 T. vinegar
Salt and pepper to taste
Crush and place among chicken pieces:
3–4 cloves garlic
Add and simmer until tender:
2 c. water
Spoon over all:
2 T. soy sauce
Sprinkle over top:
1 t. oregano
Cook until most of the liquid is absorbed and chicken is browned (about 30–40 minutes). Delicious served with steamed rice.

—Marilyn Smith
Souderton, Pennsylvania

Hospitality—an Act of Faith

In Luke's Gospel we have the wonderful Emmaus story. Two distinguished disciples are walking along the road to Emmaus. They meet a stranger and tell him about their sorrow and the death of all their hopes. The stranger, who is Jesus, then begins to tell them why the Messiah had to suffer. When they come to an inn, the disciples persuade him to eat with them and only when eating together do they recognize him as their crucified Lord. Only in breaking the bread of hospitality did their confusion turn to hope....

To welcome the stranger is an act of faith. That is why St. Benedict stresses, as he does, hospitality to guests. The stranger is not just a person, but all the ambiguity, the unknown, the otherness in life. Faith can help us greet this otherness not as a threat, but as a possible gift. God is the ultimate stranger, unpredictable, potentially threatening our security. Faith is the attitude of one who searches the face of every stranger and guest looking for God.

—Benedictine Sisters of Perpetual Adoration,
"Hospitality," November 23, 2001

Tandoori Chicken
India

Tandoori Murghi
(ton-DOOR-ee MUR-gee)

Serves 6

Place in 9"x13" lightly greased baking pan:
- **12 pieces of chicken**

Blend in blender:
- **2 large onions, sliced**
- **2 cloves garlic**
- **3 T. oil**
- **1 cup yogurt**
- **2 T. lemon juice**
- **1 t. salt**
- **1 T. ground coriander**
- **1 T. ground cumin**
- **½ t. ground ginger**
- **1 t. turmeric**
- **½ t. cinnamon**
- **¼ t. cayenne pepper**
- **¼ t. black pepper**
- **1 T. curry powder**

Pour over chicken and marinate 4 hours in refrigerator. Bake at 375° F. for 50 minutes. Serve with fluffy rice and vegetables.

Variations:
(1) Tomato juice can be substituted for yogurt. (2) Quartered potatoes mixed in with chicken make a nice addition.

—*A. J. Mann*
Elizabethtown, PA (Bihar, India)
Erma Sider
Mechanicsburg, PA (Bihar, India)

Mutton Stew
United States / Navajo

'Atsi' Hahaázh Beezh

(AT-see ha-HAAZH bayzh)

Serves 8

Combine in a large soup pot:

2 lbs. mutton neck / or lamb shoulder roast
2 qt. water
2 t. salt
1 t. pepper

Cook till tender (1 hr. for shoulder roast, 2–3 for mutton neck). Remove bones. Cool to harden fat and discard. Return the meat and broth to the pot and add:

2 large onions, chopped
6 large potatoes, diced
Cabbage, squash, carrots or other vegetables may be added if available

Simmer until tender (about 20 minutes). Serve with Fry Bread (see recipe).

—Ernestine Chavez, Annabelle Yazzie, Rebecca Eldridge, and Karen Redfearn Bloomfield, NM

Liver Sausage
United States / Navajo

Mix together:

1 liver, heart, fat, and lung of a sheep or goat, ground

Add:

2 medium raw potatoes, peeled, and chopped
½ onion, chopped
2 small celery stalks, chopped
2 t. salt

Mix well. Put in a clean sheep or goat stomach, and tie with string. Place in 2½ c. water in a pan and cook slowly for one hour.

—Karen Redfearn New Mexico

Lamb Curry with Sweet Onions
India

Kheema do Pyaza
(KHEE-mah doh pee-AH-zah)

Serves 6

Heat **2 T. cooking oil** in a large, nonstick skillet. When very hot, add and sauté until golden brown:

2 very large onions, thinly sliced

Remove onions from skillet and set aside. Add **1 T. cooking oil** to same skillet and sauté until soft:

1 large green pepper, thinly sliced

Remove pepper from skillet and set aside. In same skillet, combine and sauté for 30 seconds:

2 cloves garlic, minced
1 T. fresh ginger, minced
1 jalapeno pepper, minced

Add and sauté, stirring to blend spices with meat:

2 lbs. lean lamb cut in julienne strips
1 t. ground cumin
1 t. turmeric
1 t. cinnamon
¼ t. ground cardamom
½ t. fennel seeds
½ t. dried hot red pepper (cayenne)
salt to taste

Cook over high heat until the lamb is done (5–7 minutes). Arrange the lamb on a serving platter. Return the onions and green pepper to the skillet to heat through, then spoon the mixture over the lamb. Serve with hot, fluffy rice.

—*A. J. Mann*
Elizabethtown, PA (Bihar, India)

Roast Pig Stomach
United States / Pennsylvania Dutch

Serves 6–8

Mother would make two or three of these and invite all the family to come home.

—Naomi Shenk

Combine for stuffing:
1½ lbs. ground sausage, cooked and drained
6 medium or 1 qt. potatoes, chopped
1 small onion, chopped
2 c. cabbage, shredded (optional)
Add the following seasonings as desired and mix well:
1–2 t. salt
½ t. pepper
1 t. parsley, dried
Fill with stuffing and sew shut:
1 large pig stomach, well-cleaned
Place in roasting pan. Add:
½ c. water
Cover and roast at 350° F. for 3 hours. Slice and serve with gravy made by adding flour and water to pan drippings, if desired.

—Naomi A. Shenk; Conestoga, PA
Arlene Martin; Elizabethtown, PA
Marian Bomberger; Dillsburg, PA

Toad-in-the-Hole
England

Serves 6

Prepare Yorkshire pudding batter (see recipe). Heat **1 T. cooking oil** in baking pan. Pour **Yorkshire pudding** into hot oil. Scatter over top:
1 T. chopped onion, fried or steamed (optional)
12–16 oz. sausages (can use cubed steak, any meat scraps, or fresh sausage)
Bake at 400° F. for 20–30 minutes until pudding is well-risen and browned.

—Judy Smith
London, England

Chinese Cabbage and Pork
Japan

Soak in warm water until soft, and squeeze out gently:
    1 pkg. *kikurage* (Chinese tree ears)
Fry until done:
    1 lb. pork, sliced
Add and stir-fry until barely limp:
    2–3 T. soy sauce
    1 bunch long *negi* (onions), cut on diagonal
    1 pack kikurage
    Chinese cabbage leaves, cut up
Add if desired:
    monosodium glutamate
Thicken with:
    2 T. cornstarch in about 1 c. water (depending on desired thickening)
Serve hot with rice.

—*Ruth Zook*
Mechanicsburg, PA (Japan)

Cape buffalo in Kruger National Park, South Africa. Photo © Corbis.

Quick Sweet and Sour Pork
Japan

Marinate for 30 minutes:

1 lb. thinly sliced pork

In the following marinade:

1 t. salt

1 t. soy sauce

1 t. sugar

Fry pork until brown and crisp; set aside. Cut vegetables into bite-size pieces and stir-fry in oil until crisp-tender:

1 onion

2 carrots

2 green peppers, or 1 pack sugar peas

Add meat and 16-oz. can pineapple chunks. Prepare sauce:

¾ c. sugar

⅓ c. soy sauce

⅓ c. vinegar

½ c. water

¼ c. pineapple juice

¼ c. cornstarch

Cook over low heat until thickened. Add sauce to meat and vegetables. Serve over hot rice.

—Ruth Zook
Mechanicsburg, PA (Japan)

Stuffed Pork Roast
Denmark

Serves 8-10

Preheat oven to 350° F. Drain and pat dry:

8 pitted prunes, soaked in hot water or apple cider

Sprinkle with lemon juice and add to prunes:

1 tart apple, peeled, cored, and diced

Select a:

3½–4 lb. boned, center-cut pork loin

With sharp knife, cut a slit down the length of the loin to make a pocket reaching almost end to end. Season with:

2 t. thyme

salt and pepper to taste

Stuff the pocket with the prunes and apple, then sew up the pocket with kitchen thread. In a casserole just big enough to hold the loin, over medium heat, melt:

1 T. butter

1 T. cooking oil

Brown the roast on all sides, adding more oil if needed. When it's brown all around, pour off fat and add:

¾ cup chicken broth

Whisk in:

½ cup heavy cream (or substitute half-and-half or sour cream)

Bring to simmer and cover. Move the casserole to the oven and bake until tender (75–90 minutes). Remove to platter and let rest.

Sauce:

Meanwhile, on top of stove, skim the fat from cooking liquid and bring to boil. Reduce the liquid to about a cup and add:

1 T. currant jelly

Simmer until dissolved and smooth. Slice roast and serve with sauce.

Pork Chops in Tomato Sauce
Honduras

Chuleta en Salsa de Tomate
(chew-LAY-tah en SAHL-sa day toh-MAH-tay)

Remove fat from **8 large pork chops** and rub with **salt**. Heat **1 T. cooking oil** in a frying pan and add the chops with:

> **1 whole clove garlic, minced**

Brown on both sides and remove from heat. In bottom of greased casserole, place:

> **5 tomatoes, peeled and chopped**
> **½ c. olives, sliced**
> **1 T. flour**
> **1 t. salt**
> **pepper to taste**

Top with browned pork chops and garlic. Pour 2 T. of the oil used to brown the chops over the meat. Bake at 400° F. for about 1 hour. Garnish with parsley.

> —*Yolanda Calderón de Herrera*
> *Tegucigalpa, Honduras*

Ham Loaf
United States / Pennsylvania Dutch

Serves 8

Mix well in a large mixing bowl:

> **2 lbs. ham, ground**
> **2 lbs. fresh lean pork, ground**
> **¾ c. saltine crackers, crushed**
> **¼ c. onions, chopped**
> **3 eggs**
> **1 c. milk**
> **1 T. chopped parsley**

Shape into 2 loaves and put in 9"x5"x3" pans. Combine for syrup to baste or glaze:

> **½ c. brown sugar**
> **¼ c. cider vinegar**
> **1 t. dry mustard**

Boil the syrup for 1 minute and pour over loaves. Bake the loaves at 350° F. for 1½ hours, basting three times.

> —*Anna Ruth Ressler*
> *Elizabethtown, PA*
> *Martha Wingert*
> *Franklin County, PA*

Relish
Zambia

Cut in pieces and fry in **1 T. cooking oil**:
    2 lbs. meat (beef, pork, or chicken)
Add when meat is brown:
    1 medium onion, diced
    1 t. salt
    3 medium tomatoes, diced
Cook until vegetables are soft. Add **2 cups water** and simmer for 30 minutes.

—Mrs. L. Hamaseele
Choma, Zambia

Ham and Potato Casserole
Québec

Casserole au Jambon et aux Pommes de Terre
(kass-ROHL oh jah-BOHN ayt oh PAHM de TAYR)

Serves 6

Québec families often serve hot full meals at noon, a reminder of their rural roots. Most children return home from school for this important meal.

Cook in boiling water for 5 minutes:
    2½ lbs. or 6 c. raw potatoes, sliced
    1 c. onions, sliced
    2 c. water
    1 t. salt
Cook and cube:
    2 c. ham
Combine for sauce:
    10-oz. can cream of mushroom soup
    1 c. milk
    1 T. prepared mustard
    1 T. parsley, chopped
    ¼ t. pepper
In 9"x13" greased pan, layer half of potatoes and onions, half of cubed ham, and half of the sauce. Repeat layers. Garnish with buttered bread cubes. Bake at 375° F. for 35–40 minutes.

—Lucie Boulanger
Romuald, Québec

Wild Boar Stew
Japan

Inoshishi
(een-oh-SHEE-shee)

Fry in oil:
 3½ oz. pork per person
Cut into bite-size pieces and add:
 ***satoimo* (taro)**
 ***gobo* (burdock)**
 ***kabu* (small round turnips)**
 long onions or leeks
 carrots
 tofu
 shiitake mushrooms
Add and cook until vegetables are soft:
 2 T. soy sauce
 2 T. sugar
 2 T. sake
 pinch of monosodium glutamate (optional) and enough water to make broth
Add:
 ½ c. *miso* (crushed soybeans) mixed with
 ⅓ c. milk
Heat through but do not boil the *miso*. Serve with rice.

Variation:
This stew also can be made with rabbit, but I usually use thinly sliced pork. Start with about 3½ oz. pork per person and include a variety of vegetables.

—*Ruth Zook*
Mechanicsburg, PA (Japan)

Shepherd's Pie
England

Serves 6

Scrub, cook, and peel:

2 lbs. potatoes

Slice thin two of the potatoes and set aside. Mash the rest, season with salt and pepper to taste, and mix with:

1 c. milk

2 T. butter

meat mixture [below]

In 2 T. cooking oil, sauté:

1 c. onion, chopped

1 lb. meat (beef, lamb, or mixed veal and pork), ground

3 cloves garlic, cut fine

Drain excess fat. Add part of:

1 c. broth

Sprinkle 1 T. flour or corn starch on top, slowly add remaining broth and simmer to a rich sauce, adding the following flavorings to taste:

1 T. tomato concentrate or paste (optional)

1 T. Worcestershire sauce or 1½ t. wine vinegar

¼ t. thyme

½ t. salt

¼ t. black pepper

Cayenne pepper (optional)

Pour into a 10" round baking dish. Spread mashed potatoes on top and, with the slices, make a ring around the edge. Sprinkle with **2 T. Parmesan cheese or grated cheddar**. Heat at 375° F. for about 20–30 minutes. Increase heat a few minutes to brown cheese.

Variation:

Add frozen peas or carrots to the meat mixture to stretch it.

> —*Judy Smith*
> *London, England*

Boiled Potatoes and Meat
Japan

Niku Jaga
(nee-koo JAH-gah)

Serves 6

Slice into thin strips and saute in **1 T. cooking oil** until browned:

½ lb. beef or pork

Add and sauté a little more:

10 small potatoes, peeled and quartered
1 small onion, thinly sliced

Add and boil gently, skimming off foam, if it forms, until potatoes are done (most of liquid should be gone):

2 c. water
1 T. sugar
2 T. Japanese soy sauce
1 t. hondashi (optional)
3 T. sake (Japanese rice wine, optional)
1 1. mirin (Japanese sweet wine, optional)

This dish is tastier if you prepare it in the morning, allow it to cool to room temperature, and then reheat for a quick evening meal. Serve with rice and a salad.

—*Dora Kawate*
Dillsburg, PA (Tokyo, Japan)

Japanese Meatballs
Japan

Niku Dango
(nee-koo DAN-goh)

Serves 6

Mix:

1 lb. ground meat (beef or mix of beef and pork)
1 onion, finely minced
2 T. Japanese soy sauce
1 T. sugar
1 t. salt
2 T. cornstarch
2 T. ginger root, finely minced

Form meat mixture into 1" balls. In frying pan, brown quickly on all sides with a little vegetable oil. Boil the following, then drop meatballs into sauce:

1½ c. water
1 T. sugar
2 T. soy sauce

Boil meat balls 10 minutes. Thicken with **1 T. cornstarch** dissolved in **¼ c. cold water**. Tasty with hot rice and a green or yellow vegetable. It's easier to make nicely shaped meatballs if your hands are wet.

—*Dora Kawate*
Dillsburg, PA (Tokyo, Japan)

Country Loaf
Québec

Pain de Compagne
(PAN dew cam-PAN-yeh)

Makes 35 slices

Cover bottom of loaf pan (9"x5"x3") with half of:

½ lb. uncooked bacon

Mix together:

1½ lbs. ground pork
1½ lbs. ground veal
1 c. fine bread crumbs
2 cloves garlic, minced
¼ c. onion, finely chopped
½ c. parsely, chopped
2 eggs, lightly beaten
1 t. thyme
2 t. salt
½ t. pepper

Press lightly in bacon-layered pan. Cover with rest of bacon. Bake at 375° F. for 1½–2 hours. Cool and remove from pan. Refrigerate and slice cold. The flavor improves if made in advance. Serve in slices with soft or toasted bread (long thin French bread is preferred). Freezes well.

—*Therese Baillargeon*
Maurice, Québec

Hiking in Mount Robson Provincial Park, British Columbia. Photo © Ron Watts/Corbis.

Multi-Meat Pie
Québec

Cipaille
(see-PIE-yeh)

In earlier days, the Québecois used meat, potatoes, and carrots as the main elements of their diet, reflecting the harsh winter climate and short growing season.

Cover bottom and sides of a casserole dish with pie crust. Mix the following ingredients, place in pie crust, and cover with top pie crust:

¾ lb. pork, cubed (uncooked)
½ lb. veal, cubed (uncooked)
½ lb. beef, cubed (uncooked)
¾ lb. cooked chicken, cubed (or turkey or caribou)
5 potatoes, cubed (uncooked)
1 large onion, chopped
1 t. chicken bouillon concentrate (powder and / or liquid)
1 t. beef bouillon concentrate
1 T. parsley
1–2 cloves garlic, minced
1 t. salt (or to taste)
½ t. pepper (or to taste)
1½ c. carrots, sliced (optional)

Bake at 250° F. for 6 hours. Serve as an evening meal. Flavor is enhanced if prepared in advance and served, after reheating, the next day.

—*Sylvie St. Hilaire*
Beauport, Québec

An Embarrassing Moment

It was our first Christmas dinner at Barjora, India, with our new friends—about forty members of the local community. We had planned the meal carefully. Fortunately, this was the sweet-potato season. The small white variety were plentiful and cheap.

Happy smiles greeted our call to come to the table, but soon the mood changed. It was just a little too quiet and the sweet potatoes were scarcely touched. Little did we realize that we had placed our guests in an awkward position.

Later we learned that the Indians consider sweet potatoes to be poor man's food. In the part of India where we lived, few people would be seen eating, much less serving, sweet potatoes.

—*Phyllis and Arthur Pye*

Salty Pie
Brazil

*This recipe demonstrates
how Brazilians use
leftovers.*

Mix together:
   **1½ c. flour
   3 eggs
   ½ stick margarine
   1½ c. milk
   1 c. grated cheese
   1 t. baking powder
   1 t. salt**

Place half mixture into buttered 8"x8" baking dish. Make a layer of whatever you have leftover (hardboiled eggs, for example, or cooked meat, onions, sweet peppers, olives, vegetables of any kind, etc.). Cover with remaining batter mixture and bake at 350° F. for about ½ hour. (*Note*: Recipe is elastic, depending on quantity of leftovers.)

Scandinavian Hash
Sweden

Serves 4

Melt **1½ T. butter** in frying pan and sauté until golden brown
   2 medium onions, sliced or chopped
Put onions on a plate and keep them hot. Add the 1½ T. butter to the pan and sauté until they begin to brown:
   1½ lbs. cold boiled or canned potatoes, diced
Add to the potatoes:
   1 lb. cooked meat, dried
Cook for another 2–3 minutes. Add sautéed onions to pan, season with salt and pepper, and heat through before serving.

Meat Pie
Québec

Pâté la Viande
(pay-TAY ah lah vee-AHND)

Makes 4–5 9" pies

This meat pie is traditional Québecois holiday fare at "réveillons," the midnight suppers served buffet style on Christmas Eve and New Year's Eve.

Prepare pastry for 4–5 2-crust 9" pies. Mix in a medium-size kettle:

> **3 lbs. ground pork or 1½ lbs. each of ground pork and ground beef or veal**
> **1 large Spanish onion, chopped**
> **1 t. salt**
> **1 large garlic clove, minced**
> **1 t. savory**
> **½ t. ground cloves**

Add water until meat is barely covered and simmer 2 hours (most of the water should cook away). Add to meat mixture so it holds together:

> **fresh bread, broken into pieces (without crust)**

Pour cooked pork mixture into pastry-lined pans and cover with pastry. Bake at 375° F. until tops are browned. (Milk brushed on top just before baking makes the tops golden.)

> —*Patti Miller*
> *St. Romuald, Québec*

Norway's popular shopping center, Ostbanehallen, on a busy street in Oslo. Photo © Corbis.

Enchiladas
United States / Navajo

Serves 10

Brown in a skillet:
> **¾ lb. hamburger (or use chicken cooked and boned)**
> **1 c. onion, chopped**

When onion is clear, drain the fat, add the following ingredients, and simmer 15 minutes:
> **1 clove of garlic, minced or mashed**
> **2 medium green chilies, skinned and chopped (may use canned)**
> **¾ c. ripe olives, chopped**
> **1 t. salt**

Remove from heat and add:
> **16-oz. jar picante sauce**

Heat in **2 T. cooking oil** to soften (1 tortilla at a time):
> **10 corn tortillas, about 5" diameter**

Put about ⅓ c. meat and sauce on each tortilla. Sprinkle grated cheddar cheese on top. Heat at 350° F. about 10 minutes until the cheese melts.

Variations:
(1) Pour half the sauce in an ungreased baking dish. Place about ⅓ c. of meat mixture on each tortilla and roll to enclose filling. Place the flap side down in the sauce in the bottom of the dish. Pour the remaining sauce evenly over the tortillas. Cover with grated cheese. Bake uncovered at 350° until thoroughly heated. (2) Cream of chicken or cream of mushroom soup may be added to the meat sauce along with chopped tomatoes, red peppers, and vinegar.

—Ernie Francisco
Bloomfield, NM

Shrimp and Ground Pork Toast
Thailand

In a bowl, mix:
- ½ c. ground pork
- ½ c. shrimp, shelled, cleaned and minced
- 1 T. spring onion and coriander, finely chopped
- 1 t. garlic salt
- ½ t. pepper
- 1 egg

Take 10 slices of stale bread. Cut in desired shapes (triangles or use cookie cutter). Spread the meat mixture over each piece of bread. Deep fry in **1 c. vegetable oil** with meat mixture side down; turn over and continue cooking for 2 more minutes until brown. Drain on paper towel. Serve hot with **2 T. of hot sauce**.

—Wannee Thompson
Manorom, Thailand

Sardine Bake
England

Serves 4

Arrange in a well-greased baking dish:
- **1½ lbs. sardines (bones and heads removed)**

Sprinkle over sardines:
- **salt and pepper to taste**
- **1 t. grated nutmeg**

Cover with a layer of:
- **3 tomatoes, skinned and sliced**

Sprinkle over the above:
- **1 onion, grated**
- **2 T. dry bread crumbs**

Pour 2 oz. melted butter over the above. Preheat oven to 350° F. Bake for 15–20 minutes or until the fish is cooked and flakes easily. Serve with fresh bread.

—Judy Smith
London, England

Hospitality in Brazil

Menus in Brazil are filled with seafood dishes, tropical fruits, and exotic flavorings. But Brazilian food also bears the imprint of outside influences. Portugal was heavily involved in West Indian trading and importing African and West Indian slaves, so with these foreigners came their foods and recipes. Creole cooking often features coconut milk (squeezed from freshly picked nuts), dried shrimp, hot malagueta peppers, avocado, and ground nuts. Then immigrants from China introduced the nation to curry, spices, lamb, stir-fries, vegetable stews, and rice dishes.

Brazilian people seem to have a weakness for tasty morsels that can be consumed in one or two bites. Thus, at any public event, food-sellers peddle everything from tiny pastries stuffed with meat or cheese to fried balls of salt cod. In most markets it's easy to find sweet treats with picturesque names such as "Longings" (see recipe) or "Angels' Cheeks."

Travel in Brazil is especially exciting at mealtimes. One visitor reported, "We stopped to eat at one place and the man had caught an armadillo, chopped it up with his machete, and threw it—shell and all—into a pot to serve us stew. We skipped it." Travelers may be offered beef lungs or chicken soup with the entire chicken in it, feet floating with the rice. One man reported that piranha fish are very popular in the Amazon region, and in spite of the many, many small bones, natives usually manage to eat the entire fish (except the head).

Brazil is the world's largest grower and the biggest consumer of beans—black ones, brown ones, red and white ones. The small black beans (*feijao preto*) are the most prized. Beans and rice are eaten by most families every day (see recipe).

Brazilians have a sweet tooth. One visitor to Copacabana tells of eating in the Le Meridien Hotel at breakfast and being served a dozen ripe tropical fruits, rich caramel *pudim*, coconut *flan* (*quindao*), succulent breads with cornmeal, banana, and coconut, and a marvelous type of preserves called *cocadas* (caramelized beets, carrots, pineapple, and a half-dozen other delicacies).

Former missionary Dondeena Caldwell says, "Years ago when I traveled the Trans-Amazon highway—little more than a red dirt slash through the jungle—I ate in primitive roadside restaurants under thatched roofs. The standard menu was a mound of starches piled one on top of the other: spaghetti, rice, potatoes, and beans baptized in meat sauce. The topping was always *farina*—another starch made from the manioc root—ground up, tossed, and gritty."

Chili Beans
United States / Navajo

This dish originated in Mexico but is a favorite of the Navajo people.

Soak overnight and cook until tender:
  3 c. dry pinto beans
In another pan, brown:
  1 lb. hamburger
Then add and cook until golden:
  ½ c. onions, chopped
Add:
  2 c. whole tomatoes
  1–2 T. red chili peppers
  2 t. salt
Simmer for 15 minutes and add:
  2 medium-size green chilies (broil or roast, skin, seed, and chop)
Drain the beans, reserving the liquid, then add them to the tomato mixture along with 2 c. of the reserved liquid. Cover and simmer for an hour.

—Faye Francisco
Bloomfield, NM

Black Beans
Venezuela

Frijoles Negros
(Free-HO-lays NAY-gross)

Rinse and cook in 2 qts. water for 2 minutes:
  2 c. (1 lb.) black beans
Cover kettle, remove from heat, and let sit for 1 hour. Drain. Add 1½ quarts water to the beans and cook without salt until tender, approximately 2 hours. Do not drain after cooking. Season with:
  1 onion, chopped
  1 small red or green sweet pepper, chopped
  1 clove garlic, minced, or garlic powder to taste
  cumin to taste (optional)
  salt
  several sprigs fresh cilantro (optional)
Continue cooking until flavor has penetrated beans, approximately ½ hour. Beans should be very soft and the juice thick. Serve with rice. This can be prepared a couple of days in advance and reheated.

—Thata Book
Manheim, PA (Cagua, Venezuela)

Puree of Brown Beans
Brazil

Tutu a Mineira
(TOO-too ah
min-EAR-uh)

Wash, drain, then put in a saucepan and cover with fresh water:

> **1½ c. kidney beans (Brazilians use native brown beans)**

Bring to boil, skimming off any scum that rises. (Don't add salt just now; it would make the beans tough.) Turn down the heat and simmer for about 2 hours or until the beans are tender. Beans vary in cooking time with quality and age, so cook longer if they're still hard. In a frying pan, sauté until soft:

> **1 onion, minced**
> **2 T. olive oil**

Add:

> **1 green bell pepper, seeded and chopped**

Cook 5 minutes more. Add:

> **2 garlic cloves, crushed**

Cook for 1 minute, then stir in:

> **2 tomatoes, skinned, seeded, and chopped**

Cook a few minutes more. Stir in:

> **¾ c. cassava meal (If unavailable, try cornmeal, but it's not the same!)**
> **2 c. cooking liquid from beans**

Mix until smooth, adding seasoning to taste. Using a slotted spoon, remove the beans from their pot. Puree them in a blender, in batches, adding a little of the reserved liquid to make a smooth puree. In a large pan, mix together the pureed beans and the cassava-meal mixture, adding enough bean cooking liquid to give a texture that is neither too stiff nor too soupy. Check the seasoning. Stand this pan in a larger pan of simmering water to prevent burning or sticking. Heat for 15 minutes so the flavors blend and the mixture thickens. You can leave it to simmer longer, but replenish the liquid as necessary. Sprinkle with chopped cilantro and scallions as you serve it. Brazilians love this dish with pork, white rice, and Crisp Stir-Fried Kale (see recipe).

Black Beans and Rice
Brazil

Fijoada
(fri-HOY-da)

Serves 6–8

In Brazil fresh oranges are favorite a side dish for beans and rice.

Wash and place in large pot with lid:
   1 lb. black beans
Cover beans with water and soak overnight. Do not drain. Add:
   1 small ham bone
   3 pepperoni sausages, cut into halves
Cover and cook 2 hours or more until the beans are tender. Salt to taste. (Consider the saltiness of the ham.) In a skillet, fry for a view minutes:
   2 medium onions, sliced
   ¼ cup lard (or olive oil)
Add:
   2 medium green peppers, cut into 5–6 wedges
   2 red pimentos, cut in quarters
Cook until tender. Remove ham bone from the beans, then and add the contents of the skillet and:
   3 pieces celery, cut 1" long
   1–2 red hot peppers (optional)
Cover and cook about 45 minutes until all is tender. The beans should be soft but not mushy. Do not drain; water used should be all absorbed. Serve over white rice.

—Dondeena Caldwell

Refried Beans
United States / Navajo

Soak overnight:
   1 lb. pinto beans
Drain beans. Add:
   6 c. water
   2 onions, chopped
   salt to taste
Cook until tender. Mash with potato masher. Hot sauce, chili powder, tomato sauce, and bacon can be added. Cook in heavy skillet until beans are thickened and juices are absorbed.

—Karen Redfearn
New Mexico

Refried Beans
Nicaragua

Frijoles Licuados
(free-HOH-lays
Lee-KWAH-dohs)

Serves 5

Liquefy in blender:
2 c. cooked pinto beans
¼ c. chopped onion
¼ c. chopped green pepper
Heat small amount of vegetable oil in frying pan. Add bean mixture and cook over low heat, stirring constantly for about 5 minutes. Add any desired seasonings such as hot sauce, salt, and chili powder. Serve with rice as part of a meal, as a dip on tortilla chips, on crackers with a little sour cream, or on crackers with an olive slice.

Variation:
Use canned red or black beans.

—*Perla Estrada*
Managua, Nicaragua

Yorkshire Pudding
England

Serves 4

Sift into a bowl:
½ c. flour
Make a well in the center and add:
2 eggs
½ t. salt
¼ c. milk
Beat gradually to a smooth batter, adding **¾ c. milk** as the mixture blends together. (Alternately, put everything into a blender and blend at top speed until smooth.) Chill for one hour. Put an 8"x8" pan into a hot oven (400°–450° F.) with **¼ c. shortening**. When very hot, add batter after stirring it several times. Although this may require baking for 30–40 minutes, check after 20 minutes. The pudding is best crisp and brown. Serve with roast beef or mutton.

—*Judy Smith*
London, England

One-Pot Meal
Nepal

Pani Roil
(PAH-nee ROH-tee)

Clean and soak overnight:
> 2 c. dried peas
> 2 c. mung peas (green gram)
> 2 c. navy beans
> 2 c. chick peas

In a heavy saucepan, heat:
> 1 T. oil
> 1 t. ground cumin
> 1 t. ground coriander
> ¼ t. black pepper.

Add and sauté lightly:
> prepared lentils (peas, etc.)
> 4 large potatoes, sliced

Add:
> 3 c. water
> 1 t. salt

Cover and simmer gently for about 15 minutes. Add and simmer gently 2–3 minutes:
> 1 package spinach, chopped
> ½ t. turmenc

While above is cooking, prepare pastry as follows. Knead:
> 1 c. whole wheat flour
> 2–3 T. water or enough to dampen and form in a ball

Knead for 2–3 minutes and roll out thin (like potpie). Cut in small squares. Make sure there is enough water in the stew, then drop in the squares separately. Boil for another 15 minutes or so, until the dough is cooked.

—*Esther Lenhert*
Kathmandu, Nepal

Hummus
Jordan

Tahini *is a thick paste made of ground sesame seeds.*

Mash thoroughly:
   15½-oz. can chickpeas, drained
Add slowly to above:
   1 c. *tahini*
   1 c. lemon juice
Mix well. *Hummus* is served in a bowl or plate and drizzled with olive oil with a few whole chickpeas for garnish. Each person tears off a bite-size piece of pita bread from the whole round piece, scoops up some *hummus* with the bread and enjoys!

Variations:
Substitute peanut butter for *tahini* as it gives a little different flavor. Use baking soda if cooking dried peas. Salt may be added as desired.

—*Ethel Kreider*
Lancaster, PA (Jordan)

Hominy and Chick Peas
Zimbabwe

Isimoni
(eh-sih-MOH-nee)

Serves 4

Combine in saucepan and bring to a boil:
   1 c. hominy grits
   2 c. canned chick peas, drained
Stir in and simmer 35 minutes:
   ¼ c. peanut butter
   ¼ t. salt
Serve as a meat substitute.

—*Martha Mpofu*
Dekezi, Zimbabwe

Garbanzo Stew
Spain

Serves 6–8

Soak 1 lb. garbanzo beans (chickpeas) overnight. Discard soaking water. In a large soup pot, Crock-Pot®, or pressure cooker combine:

soaked beans
ham bone or hock
1 lb. Spanish sausage (*chorizo*)
1–2 slices bacon, chopped
1 onion, chopped
2 carrots, cut in chunks
1 red sweet pepper, chopped
4 cloves of garlic, peeled
½ t. paprika
1 t. salt
¼ t. pepper
water to cover

Cook until tender. Remove fat and cut meat into small pieces. Serve with fresh, hot bread.

—*A. J. Mann*
Elizabethtown, PA

A gondola rises over Rio de Janeiro, Brazil. Photo © Corbis.

161

Potato Spanish Omelet
Spain

Tortilla Española
(tor-TEE-yah
es-pan-yoh-lah)

Serves 8

Thinly slice **4–5 medium potatoes**. Heat **2 T. olive oil** in skillet to very hot. Add potatoes and cover. Check every couple of minutes to ensure they don't stick together and burn on edges. Beat in separate bowl:

6 eggs
salt and pepper to taste

As potatoes soften, add:

2 T. onions, chopped

Cook for 2–3 minutes more. Strain potatoes and add to eggs. Let sit for 15–20 minutes. Mash potatoes into egg mixture. Prepare another medium-size skillet, making it very hot. Add egg-and-potato mixture to skillet. Turn heat down right away. When it begins to thicken, flip it, using a large plate. Slide it back into the skillet. Flip 2 or 3 more times until it's firm. Serve as an appetizer by cutting it into squares and picking it up with toothpicks or as a light supper, cut in wedges and served with a salad.

—Merly Bundy
Madrid, Spain

"What Did You Say?"

We were eating a delicious supper at the home of a former student and asked what ingredients were used in the filling for the delicious boiled dumplings. Our Chinese friend intended to say, "Meat and cabbage," but got the wrong English word. She told us, "Meat and garbage"!

—Joyce Peterman
Manheim, PA

Country Omelet
France

L'Omelette a la Campagnarde
(LOM-let ah lah kam-pan-YARD)

Serves 2–3

Heat a 10" nonstick frying pan. Add 3 T. vegetable oil and fry at medium heat:

1 medium sized potato, peeled and cut into ½" thick pieces

When the potatoes are golden brown on both sides, remove from frying pan, drain on paper towels, and set aside. Then fry:

½ lb. smoked bacon, blanched in boiling water, rinsed, dried, cut into ¼" matchstick-like lengths

Fry only until the pieces begin to take on color, but don't let them get crisp, or they will be bitter in the omelet. Remove and drain on paper towels. Discard or save for another use all but 1 T. of drippings. Whisk together:

4 large fresh eggs
1 t. water
½ t. salt
½ t. pepper
2 T. coarsely chopped parsley

Add the cooked potatoes and bacon with:

1 scallion, root and part of green leaves trimmed off, coarsely chopped
½ c. fresh spinach, stemmed, well washed, and coarsely chopped

Make sure that all of the ingredients are well-coated with the egg mixture. Heat frying pan containing 1 T. of drippings and pour the mixture into it. Using wooden spatula, push potatoes toward the bottom and reduce the heat. Put the spatula into the center of the omelet, lift it a bit and allow the uncooked egg to run under it. This hastens cooking. Choose a kitchen plate that is larger than 10" and invert it over the frying pan. Holding it tightly against the frying pan, flip the pan over and leave the omelet, done side up, in the plate. Quickly slip the omelet, uncooked side down, back into the frying pan. Tidy up the edges and let omelet brown for 2–3 minutes. Invert the plate over the pan again and flip it to see that the second side is properly browned. If it's done, place on serving plate, sprinkle with **1 t. grated Parmesan cheese** and serve at once.

Eggs in a Nest
France

Les Oeufs Au Nid
(lays-UFFS oh-NEED)

Serves 4

Preheat oven to 450° F. Choose 4 individual baking dishes, butter generously, and sprinkle with Parmesan cheese. Tap out excess. Beat in a mixing bowl:

whites of 8 large fresh eggs
½ t. salt
½ t. cream of tartar

Beat these ingredients slowly at first, then more rapidly, until the whites mount in soft peaks and keep their shape. Divide the beaten whites in the 4 baking dishes and make deep impressions in the center of each. Place 2 egg yolks in each depression and spoon over each one:

1½ T. heavy cream

Pull the whites into peaks and scatter over them:

2 T. finely grated Gruyere cheese
½ t. freshly ground black pepper

Set dishes on cookie sheet and bake in oven for 10 minutes or until the meringues are golden brown. Serve while hot and the cheese is toasted and fragrant.

Grilled Cheese and Tomatoes
Malawi

Serves 4–6

Slice **4 ripe tomatoes** and arrange the slices on the oven rack. Add to the top of each slice:

1 T. grated cheese
salt and pepper to taste

Bake for 10 minutes at 400° F. or until cheese melts. (*Note*: put cookie sheet under to catch drippings from tomatoes.) Garnish with parsley. Serve immediately.

—Mel Andricks
Blantyre, Malawi

Egg Curry
India

Serves 4–6

Hard-boil and cut in half lengthwise:
  8 eggs
Sauté in **¼ c. vegetable oil** until onions are golden:
  2 medium onions, minced
  1 t. marjoram
  1 t. thyme
Add and cook, stirring constantly, for 3–4 minutes:
  1 t. turmeric
  1½ t. salt
  2 t. dried, unsweetened coconut
  1 T. curry powder
  1 T. parsley flakes
Next add:
  4 large tomatoes, sliced
  1 c. yogurt
Stir well, then add eggs, being careful not to break them.
Cover, lower heat, and allow to simmer for 10 minutes.
Serve as a main dish with rice.

—Ken Hoke
Carlisle, PA

A baker removes loaves from oven in India.

Fried Noodles Thai Style
Thailand

Heat **3 T. cooking oil** in a frying pan and sauté:

1 T. garlic, chopped
1 T. shallots, chopped

When yellow, add:

12 oz. narrow rice noodles

Fry, turning constantly with spatula to prevent sticking. Then move noodles to side or remove from pan. Heat **2–3 T. cooking oil** in pan and add:

½ c. pork, cut into small slivers
½ c. pickled white radish, chopped
1 cake soybean curd, cut into small slivers
1 t. dried chilies, ground

Return the noodles to the pan, mix thoroughly, and move to side or remove. Heat another **2 T. cooking oil** in the pan. Break into pan and scramble with spatula, spreading in a thin layer:

3 eggs

When set, return the noodles and mix together with the following sauce:

4 T. sugar
3 T. fish sauce
4 T. tamarind juice or vinegar

Add:

1 pack bean sprouts
½ c. Chinese leek leaves

Turn to mix together. Spoon onto plates and sprinkle with:

½ c. roasted peanuts, ground

—*Kathy Brubaker*
Bangkok, Thailand

German Hot Potato Salad
United States / Pennsylvania Dutch

Warmer Kartoffelsalat
(VEHR-mer ker-TOFF-el sah-laht)

Serves 10–12

Boil, peel, and slice thinly:

12 medium potatoes in jackets

In skillet, fry until crisp:

12 slices of bacon

Remove bacon and drain on paper towel. Crumble and set aside. Save drippings in a one-cup measure. Sauté until golden brown:

2–3 medium onions, diced

1 t. bacon drippings

Remove onions, add to potatoes with:

1 c. celery, thinly sliced

parsley, snipped

To bacon drippings, add enough **salad oil** to make ½ cup. Pour into skillet. Add:

1 c. sugar

5 T. flour

2–3 t. salt

½ t. ground black pepper

1 t. celery seed

Stir until smooth. Continue cooking for 3 minutes. Pour dressing over potato mixture. Add crumbled bacon. Mix thoroughly and carefully. Keep warm until ready to serve or serve immediately at room temperature. Garnish with thinly sliced hard-boiled egg and sweet green pepper rings.

—Faithe Hoffman
Palmyra, PA

German Hot Potato Salad (Microwave Recipe)
Germany

Serves 4–6

Wash and pierce with fork:

4 medium potatoes, unpeeled

Place potatoes on paper towel in microwave oven. Microwave on high 8–10 minutes or until tender, turning over and rearranging every 4 minutes. Remove from oven, cool slightly, peel potatoes and cut into 1" slices to make about 4 cups. Cut into small pieces:

6 slices bacon

Place the bacon in 2-qt. casserole and cover with paper towel. Microwave on high about 6 minutes, stirring after 3 minutes, until crisp. With slotted spoon, remove bacon to paper towels to drain. Set aside. Stir into bacon fat until smooth:

2 T. flour
¼ c. sugar
1½ t. salt
⅛ t. pepper
½ t. celery seed

Microwave on high 1–2 minutes until bubbly, stirring after 1 minute. Add to flour mixture:

1 c. water
½ c. vinegar

Microwave on high for 4 minutes until mixture boils and thickens, stirring after 1 minute. Remove from oven and stir smooth. Add potatoes, bacon, and:

1 bunch green onions, cleaned, cut in small pieces, using ¼" of the green tops

Stir gently so potatoes hold their shape. Cover casserole and let stand until ready to serve.

—Barbara Glatzel

Crumbs
Colombia

Serves 4–6

This is a common breakfast for some regions of Colombia. Serve with tossed salad and fruit.

Soak **4–6 tortillas** in **1–2 c. milk** (or just enough to soak tortillas well) for at least 30 minutes or until they fall apart easily. With your hands, divide these into small pieces and continue to soak in the milk. In a skillet, fry in small amount of oil:
>   **1 onion, finely chopped**
>   **3 tomatoes, finely chopped**

Cook until most of the liquid of the tomatoes is gone. Beat **4–6 eggs** and mix with tortilla / milk mixture. Add this mixture to skillet and cook. Add salt to taste.

Variations:
(1) Other types of breads can be used in place of tortillas.
(2) Garlic powder and hot sauce are optional.

—*Tatiana Mallarino Giraldo*
Bogota, Colombia

Cornmeal
Porridge
Zambia

Insima
(en-SHEE-mah)

Serves 4–6

Bring **4 c. water** to a boil in large heavy saucepan. Slowly add to the boiling water:
>   **1 c. cornmeal mixed with 1 c. water**

As you add the cornmeal mixture, stir vigorously with a wooden spoon to keep from getting lumps. Slowly add **another ½–1 c. cornmeal** to the mixture on the stove, stirring vigorously and continuously with wooden spoon. When cornmeal mixture seems very thick, it is time to stop adding more cornmeal. Cover and simmer ½–¾ hour, stirring occasionally and vigorously with wooden spoon. It is ready to eat when it no longer tastes like raw cornmeal. *Note*: Zambians do not put salt in their *insima*, because they heavily salt the chicken or other relish eaten with it.

—*Ardys E. Thuma*
Bradford, OH (Choma, Zambia)

Cornmeal Porridge
Zimbabwe

Sadza
(SUH-dzah) or
Isitshwala
(eh-seh-CHWAH-lah)

Serves 4

This is the staple dish served in Zimbabwe and may be served twice a day.

Boil in saucepan:
> **3 c. water**

Combine in a bowl:
> **1 c. white cornmeal**
> **1 c. cold water**

Stir mixture into boiling water. Stir constantly until porridge boils and thickens. Cover, lower heat, and cook for 5–10 minutes. Add gradually while stirring:
> **½ c. dry cornmeal**

Stir porridge constantly to keep it smooth. Cover and simmer for an additional 5–10 minutes. Serve with Zimbabwean Stew, Peanut Butter Gravy, Cabbage with Peanut Butter or any similiar recipe.

> —*Boitatelo Mguni*
> *Zimbabwe*
> *Fadzai Moyo*
> *London, U.K.*

Mixed Grain Dish
Zimbabwe

Soak overnight:
> **1 c. raw peanuts**

Drain water, add fresh water to cover peanuts, cook for about 2 hours. Then add:
> **2 c. hominy**
> **1 c. kidney beans, canned**
> **1 c. chickpeas, canned**
> **½ t. salt**

Simmer gently for 15–20 minutes. Serve as main course of the meal with vegetable or salad.

> —*Beatrice Ncube*
> *Dekezi, Zimbabwe*

Spanish Paella
Spain

Heat ½ c. **olive oil** in heavy pan and sauté until brown:
2–3 lbs. chicken pieces, cut in small pieces
Set aside. Then sauté in the same pan, stirring frequently:
6 large shrimp, shelled and deveined
Remove from pan and reserve. Steam in a little water until they open, then drain, reserving juices:
12 mussels in shells, scrubbed
12 small clams in shells, scrubbed
In remaining oil, sauté:
1 large onion, chopped
1 clove garlic, minced
2 c. rice
Cook, lightly stirring until grains are coated with oil. Put rice in a shallow 12"x14" paella pan. As evenly as possible arrange shrimp and chicken over the rice. Add:
1 tomato, peeled and chopped
10-oz. package of frozen peas
Measure clam and mussel broth and add enough water to make 4½ c. Pour into a saucepan and add:
5 c. chicken broth
Bring to a boil. Stir in:
2 t. salt to taste
½ t. ground saffron
Heat the paella pan and pour the hot broth over the rice. Cook over moderately high heat for 10 minutes. Reduce heat to medium and cook 15 minutes longer, until rice is tender and liquid is absorbed. Arrange clams and mussels, still in shells, on top.

Variation:
Add parsley and lemon juice for more flavor and zest.

—*Merly Bundy*
Madrid, Spain

Rice Quiche
Japan

Serves 4

Fry and then set aside:
> **2 slices bacon, chopped**

Fry together in bacon fat and **1–2 t. butter**:
> **1 onion, minced**
> **1 clove garlic, minced**
> **1 red pepper, chopped**
> **1 green pepper, chopped**

Mix and place in buttered baking dish:
> **2 c. cooked rice**
> **1 c. raw squash, cubed**
> **fried bacon**
> **1 T. parsley, minced**
> **¾ t. salt**
> **dash pepper / dash nutmeg (optional)**

Beat together and pour over rice mixture:
> **4 eggs**
> **1 c. evaporated milk**
> **Top with ¼ c. grated cheese**

Bake at 350° F. for about 40 minutes or until set.

—*Mariko Kogoma*
Tokyo, Japan

Fisherman stow their nets at the end of day's work in Sicily. Photo © Corbis.

Spanish Rice Pie
Spain

Serves 6–8

Cook **2 pkgs. frozen spinach** for 5 minutes and squeeze dry. Fry in **5 T. cooking oil:**
   1 clove garlic, minced
   1 medium onion, chopped
   ½ t. salt
   dash of pepper
Mix and beat lightly:
   4 eggs
   5 T. grated Italian cheese
   ¼ c. milk
   2½ T. grated mozzarella cheese
Add and mix well:
   1 c. cooked rice
   Pinch crushed red pepper
Fill a greased 10" pie pan and bake at 375° F. for ½ hour until lightly brown. Bake 10 minutes more after sprinkling **2½ T. grated mozzarella cheese** on top.

—*A. J. Mann*
Elizabethtown, PA

Spanish Rice
United States / Navajo

Serves 4

Brown and drain:
   1 lb. ground beef
Chop and brown:
   1 medium onion
   ½ green bell pepper
Add:
   1 c. rice
   1 c. tomatoes
   2 t. salt
   1 t. chili powder
   2 c. water
Cover tightly, lower heat, and cook slowly for 30 minutes or until the rice is cooked.

—*John Jarred*
Dzith na o Dilthe Le, NM

173

Lentils, Macaroni, and Rice
Egypt

Kusheri
(kush-REE)

Cook separately, adding salt to taste:
  1 c. rice
  1 c. macaroni
  1 c. lentils
In **2 t. cooking oil**, sauté and set aside for garnish:
  1 large onion, chopped
In **2 T. hot cooking oil**, sauté and set aside:
  1 large onion, chopped
  2-3 cloves garlic, minced
Add and simmer 5–10 minutes:
  3 tomatoes, chopped
  ½ t. salt
  1 c. water
  black pepper to taste, or hot red pepper
Remove from heat and add:
  1 T. vinegar
Serve in individual bowls, starting with rice, then macaroni, then lentils. Cover with tomato sauce and top with sprinkling of fried onions.

—Brian and Marcelle Zook
Egypt

Rice and Lentils
Nepal

Khichidi
(KICH-i-dee)

Asafoetida *is a resinous gum exported from Iran or Afghanistan, which adds an onion-like flavor to vegetarian dishes.*

Into **5 c. boiling water**, add:
  ½ c. black gram lentils
After it reaches boiling point again, add:
  ¼ t. turmeric
  ¼ t. asafoetida
Cover and simmer until the lentils are soft (may add more water if too thick). Add:
  1 c. rice
Simmer until the rice is cooked. Add:
  1 t. oil
  ½ t. ginger
  1 t. salt
Serve hot for a nourishing but light meal.

—Esther Lenhert
Kathmandu, Nepal

Spinach and Rice Pondo
Zaire

Serves 6

Zairians enjoy this dish spicy hot.

Cook together in saucepan:

2 pkgs. frozen spinach, chopped, or the equivalent of fresh spinach, chopped
1 medium onion, chopped

Drain excess liquid. Add and stir over low heat until blended:

½ c. creamy peanut butter
2 t. hot pepper sauce—or more to taste
dash of salt

Serve as a main dish over 4–6 c. hot, cooked rice.

Variations:
Add cooked corn or any cooked meat, chopped.

—*Lucille Charlton*
Vancouver, BC (Zaire)

Rice with Red Pork
Thailand

Marinate ½ **lb. pork tenderloin** in this sauce for several hours:

6 oz. can tomato paste
1½ c. water
¼ c. soy sauce
2 T. sugar

Bake, covered, until tender. May baste and broil at end to lightly brown outside. Slice ¼" thick. Arrange pork and cucumbers attractively on plates of rice. Thicken pan juices with flour mixed with water and pour over meat and **3–4 cucumbers (sliced ¼" thick).** Garnish with **fresh coriander leaves (cilantro).** Optional sauce:

2 T. sugar
2 T. vinegar
2 T. soy sauce

Mix together and add chilies sliced into thin rings.

—*Kathy Brubaker*
Grantham, PA (Bangkok, Thailand)

Fried Rice
Central Java, Indonesia

Nasi goreng
(NAH-see goh-reng)

Serves 6

Javanese people serve this for breakfast usually at room temperature, but I like to serve it piping hot. It is great with shrimp-flavored chips available at international food stores.

Measure into rice cooker or pan:

2 c. rice
3¾–4 c. cold water

Cook rice following package directions or bring rice and water to boil in pan. Stir to loosen rice from bottom. When mixture boils, lower heat to warm. Cover. Do not peek for 20 minutes. Turn off heat, remove lid, cool, preferably for a number of hours. Rice must be cold. (Leftover rice serves the purpose.) Prepare the following ingredients for stir fry:

1 large onion, chopped
3 cloves garlic, sliced
1 c. steamed broccoli or leftover green vegetables (i.e., peas, celery)
2–3 T. cooking oil
1 deboned chicken breast, julienned
2 t. cumin
soy sauce

Pour oil into wok. Add chicken with a few slices garlic. Stir fry until no pink remains. Sprinkle **1 t. cumin** over mixture. Remove chicken. Add and stir-fry the onion, remaining garlic, 1 more t. cumin, and a shake of soy sauce. Gradually add rice (fluff with fork first to separate grains), stirring constantly. Return chicken strips to wok. Add green vegetables, soy sauce to taste. Stir-fry until heated through and serve piping hot.

Suggested optional garnishes:

2 shallots, sliced and fried
½–1 t. red hot pepper paste, stirring into fried rice at end
1 egg sheet

Prepare egg sheet as follows: Beat egg and pour into wok, tipping wok to make thin sheet as it fries in a bit of oil. Lift with spatula, roll up, slice ¼" wide.

—Shirlee Kohler Yoder
Harrisonburg, VA
(Central Java, Indonesia)

Mashed Potatoes
Egypt

Boil, peel, and mash:
   6 potatoes
Add and mix thoroughly:
   1 c. milk
   pinch of salt and pepper
   2 eggs
In a skillet, fry:
   1 large onion, diced.
Add and cook until brown:
   2 lbs. ground beef
   pinch of salt and pepper
Beat and set aside:
   1 egg
Put half of potato mixture in baking pan. Cover with a layer of meat mixture. Then add the other half of the potato mixture and top with the beaten egg. Bake at 350° F. for 45 minutes or until brown.

—*Brian and Marcelle Zook*
Egypt

Broccoli Pasta
Italy

Serves 4

This is great served with Italian sausage!!

Boil thoroughly in a large pot:
   1 bunch broccoli, washed and cut
When finished, strain broccoli and save the water to cook pasta. (This gives pasta more flavor.) While water is reheating for pasta, heat in a small saucepan a small amount of virgin olive oil. Sauté on low heat until golden in color:
   2 garlic cloves
Pureé the broccoli, oil, and garlic in a food processor. Cook according to package directions:
   1 lb. pasta
When pasta is cooked al dente, drain, retaining 1 c. of pasta water. Place the pasta in a large bowl. Mix in broccoli pureé and remaining pasta water until smooth. Top with **Parmesan cheese** and serve hot.

—*Krista Huck*

177

Potato Dumplings
Brazil

Nhoques-Especials
(NO-qways es-PEH-see-als)

Serves 6–8

Press through a ricer or mash:
2 lbs. potatoes, peeled, cooked in salted water
Then add:
1 T. butter
1 egg
1 t. salt
1½ c. cornstarch
dash of nutmeg
Sprinkle flour on a breadboard and let above mixture rest on board for 10 minutes. Divide the dough into 4 sections, roll each up like a jelly roll, and cut into 1–2" pieces. Drop into salted water, almost boiling. When the dumplings are done, they will rise to top. Remove and put into top of double boiler to keep warm.

Fry in a saucepan with a minimum amount of cooking oil:
1 clove garlic
1 medium onion, chopped
2 lbs. ripe tomatoes, peeled and chopped
Season with salt and pepper, to taste. Move dumplings to 9"x13" baking dish. Combine the tomato sauce with **1 lb. hamburger** that has been cooked well-done and drained thoroughly, then pour this over dumplings. Sprinkle on top:
3–4 green onions, chopped
½ cup grated cheese (Cheddar or Jack)
Bake at 350° F. until cheese is well melted.

Stuffed Mashed Potato Dumplings
Russia

Serves 6

Cut into 1" cubes:

1 lb. lean pork

Season with salt, pepper, and 1 t. sugar. Sauté in butter 30 minutes, until tender. Remove from pan and let cool. Boil in salted water:

9–10 medium potatoes, peeled

Drain potatoes and press through a ricer. Mix well with:

1 c. hot milk

1 T. sour cream

1 egg

3 T. flour

salt to taste

Shape the warm potato mixture into dumplings approximately 2½" in diameter and stuff each one with a piece of sautéed pork. Dip dumplings into **2 beaten eggs,** coat with ⅔ **c. bread crumbs**, and place on a carefully greased baking sheet. Bake until brown in a 450° F. oven for 5–10 minutes. Cover with:

1 c. sour cream

Return dumplings to oven for 5 minutes more. Serve with mushroom or tomato sauce and salad.

The Russian Orthodox Cathedral of St. Basil the Blessed, Moscow. Photo © Corbis.

Baked Stuffed Zucchini
Egypt

Macaroni Cosa Bishemal
(MAK-a-ROW-nah coh-SAH bish-eh-MALL)

Serves 8

In Egypt, bishemal *is usually eaten as a main meal with salad as a side dish.*

Make a white sauce using:

¼ c. oil or butter
3 T. flour
salt and pepper to taste
2 c. milk

Cook gently until thick, then allow to cool. Cook in boiling water until soft on the inside, but not well done:

8 medium-to-large zucchini

Slice zucchini lengthwise and remove middle. Brush 9"x13" pan with oil and put 8 halves in the pan. Fill each half with the following meat mixture cooked well:

1 medium onion, chopped and fried in 1–2 T. cooking oil
1 lb. beef, minced
salt and pepper to taste (optional: hot pepper, cumin, parsley, paprika)

When stuffed, cover each zucchini with the other half. Add to sauce and mix well:

2 eggs

Cover the zucchini with white sauce. Bake at 350° F. until brown.

Variations:
Cooked macaroni can be substituted for the zucchini. Add 1 can of crushed tomatoes to minced beef and cook until tomatoes are thick and dark. Layer macaroni and the meat / tomato mixture. Top with white sauce and bake until brown.

—*Amal*
Egypt

Hearty Eggplant Parmesan
Italy

Serves 8

Cut lengthwise into ½" slices:

3 eggplants (1½ lbs. each), having cut off the stems and bottoms

Sprinkle both sides of the eggplant halves with **coarse salt.** Layer slices horizontally in colander and cover loosely with plastic wrap. Weigh down the plastic with a heavy bowl. Set colander over a jelly-roll pan or in sink and let drain for 2 hours. Rinse eggplant well under cold running water. Firmly press slices between layers of paper towel until eggplant looks light green and translucent, leathery to touch. Arrange oven racks in the center and bottom positions; preheat oven to 475° F. Grease 2 large baking sheets with **1½ t. cooking oil** each. On a plate, combine:

½ c. grated Parmesan cheese
¾ c. fine, dry bread crumbs
½ t. pepper

Beat in a bowl:

3 large egg whites
3 T. water

Working in batches, dip eggplant slices in egg whites, then in crumb mixture to coat. Arrange on prepared baking sheets. Drizzle with **2 T. olive oil.** Place a baking sheet on each rack and bake 8 minutes. Rotate sheets top to bottom, back to front, then bake another 8 minutes. Turn slices over and bake 16 more minutes, rotating pans at 8 minutes as before, until eggplant is browned and tender. Reduce oven to 375° F.

Spread **1 c. fat-free marinara sauce** evenly over bottom of 9"x13" casserole dish. Arrange ⅓ of eggplant slices in sauce to cover. Scatter over top:

6 oz. part-skim mozzarella cheese
¼ c. packed fresh basil leaves, torn
2 T. grated Paremesan cheese

Spread another **1 cup marinara sauce** over this. Layer another ⅓ of eggplant, then top with an equal amount of **mozzarella, basil,** and **Parmesan cheese.** Spread **1 c. marinara sauce** over the top. Layer with remaining eggplant, **1 c. marinara sauce,** then **2 T. Parmesan.** Cover with foil and bake at 375 F. for 20 minutes. Uncover and bake 15 minutes more until bubbly around edges. Let stand 15 minutes. Garnish with basil sprigs.

Stuffed Peppers
Argentina

Pimientos Rellenos
(pim-ee-EN-tohs ree-YEN-ohs)

Serves 4–8

2 T. olive oil
3 tsp salt

Prepare by cutting 1" piece from each stem end, then cutting out seeds and fibers of:

8 green peppers

Chop up 4 of the tops you have cut off. Heat **2 T. olive oil** in skillet and sauté the chopped peppers for 5 minutes with:

½ c. chopped onions

Remove from heat and mix in:

1 lb. ground beef
1½ t. salt
¼ t. black pepper
3 eggs, beaten

Then add:

1 c. canned corn
¼ c. chopped green olives

Stuff peppers with this mixture and arrange them in a baking dish. Add:

2 c. canned tomato sauce
⅛ t. dried, ground chili peppers
1½ t. salt

Cover and bake in 350° F. oven for 1¼ hours or until the peppers are tender. Remove cover for last 15 minutes of baking time.

The Sweet Taste of Hospitality

Three of us headed out on bicycles from El Carmen, Bolivia, to La Cabeza, an Indian settlement about seven kilometers away. When we arrived, we were warmly greeted by a group of women who were already making preparations for the noon meal. While they cooked, we visited with them and learned about how the women tilled their own fields of rice and beans. After we ate together, we walked out to the fields, another couple kilometers from the village.

When I left—dead tired—on my borrowed bicycle to return to El Carmen, I knew I would never see these women again. But I also knew that they had touched me in a way I would never forget. Their hospitality, offered graciously and without pretense, left me with a wonderful and lingering sweet taste of Bolivia.

—*Harriet Sider Bicksler*

Stuffed Cabbage Rolls
Russia

Serves 4–6

Preheat oven to 325° F. Prepare as follows:

1 large head cabbage

Remove the core from the cabbage head. Soak cabbage in cold water for 10 minutes. Remove 12 leaves (more if the leaves are small). Cover these leaves with boiling water. Remove from heat, let stand 10–12 minutes, then drain. Brown in a saucepan:

1 lb. hamburger

Drain and add:

1 cup finely chopped onion
1 cup cooked rice
½ cup tomato sauce
1 tsp. salt
pepper to taste

Mix thoroughly and simmer for 3 minutes. Put about ⅓ cup of this filling at stem ends of each leaf. (Put less if leaves are small.) Roll up tightly, tucking in ends as if wrapping a package. Put seam side down in 8"x8" pan. Pour the rest of the **15-oz. can tomato sauce** over cabbage rolls. Bake at 325° F. for 45 minutes.

Alternative Russian sauce:

Brown ½ **c. chopped onions** in **4 t. butter** or cooking oil. Stir in **2–3 medium tomatoes** that have been peeled, seeded, and chopped. Add dash of **salt and pepper**. Add ½ **c. sour cream** mixed with **1 t. flour**. Pour this over cabbage and bake.

—*Mary Faducovich Hart*

Stuffed Cabbage
Germany

Serves 6

Preheat oven to 350° F. Cook covered in boiling water for 5–7 minutes:

1 head green cabbage

Plunge into cold water and separate leaves. Return head to boiling water if needed to cook the inner leaves. Trim ribs where needed. Blanch:

¾ lb. spinach, washed and trimmed

Drain, cool, squeeze out water, and chop. Sauté in **2 T. olive oil** until tender:

1½ c. onion, chopped fine

¾ lb. white mushrooms, washed and chopped fine

Add:

4 T. garlic, minced

Cook 2–3 minutes. Add the chopped spinach and heat through. Season with salt and pepper; reserve. In another bowl, combine:

1 lb. ground sausage

2 eggs, whisked

½ c. parsley, chopped

Finally, add the reserved vegetables. In a saucepan, combine:

1½ c. beef bouillon

2 c. marinara sauce

Bring to boil, then remove from heat and reserve. Rub an ovenproof casserole with **4 T. olive oil**. Divide the sausage-and-vegetable filling into 12–16 balls. Dry cabbage leaves with paper toweling. Sprinkle the leaves with salt and pepper, then form each cabbage leaf around the mixture that has been made into balls. Place in oiled casserole dish. Pour marinara sauce mixture around and over cabbage balls. Cover and bake 45 minutes. Sprinkle with parsley to serve.

Tofu Patties
Japan

Tofu (prepared from soybeans) is an excellent source of protein. One-quarter pound is equivalent to a glass of milk or a very large egg.

In a cheesecloth bag, squeeze water from:
 2 squares tofu
Mash together in bowl with tofu:
 ½ c. carrot, minced
 ½ c. mushrooms, chopped
 1 t. salt
 1 T. sugar
 dash of Accent° seasoning
Add and mix well:
 1 beaten egg
Shape into patties and fry in enough cooking oil to cover patties. Serve with mustard and soy sauce.

—*Lucille Graybill*
Osaka, Japan

Tofu Sauce for Vegetables
Japan

On a cloth-covered cutting board, drain for ½ hour:
 1 square tofu
Place in blender with tofu:
 3 T. sesame seeds
Blend; then add the following and blend thoroughly:
 1 T. sugar
 1 t. Accent° seasoning
 1 t. soy sauce
Pour over the cooked vegetables.

—*Lucille Graybill*
Osaka, Japan

Scrambled Tofu on Rice
Japan

Place in cheesecloth bag and drain:
1 square tofu
Brown in **1 T. cooking oil**:
½ lb. ground beef
½ c. carrots, slivered
2 scallions, chopped
4–5 sprigs parsley, minced
Scramble the tofu as you add to meat and vegetables.
Then stir in:
3 T. soy sauce
½ t. salt
1 T. sugar
dash of Accent® seasoning
Add and cook until they are set:
2 slightly beaten eggs
Serve over steamed rice in bowls.

—Lucille Graybill
Lusaka, Japan

Pepian
United States / Hispanic

Fry together:
1 lb. tomatoes, chopped
1 chili pepper, sliced
1 medium onion, chopped
2 cloves garlic, minced
Toast together:
½ oz. sesame seed
½ oz. rice
3 whole cloves or ¼ t. ground cloves
5 peppercorns
1 stick cinnamon or 1 t. ground cinnamon
3 slices of bread toasted until they are a little burned (to give a dark color)
Mix all the above in a blender, then heat gently in a saucepan with **1 t. cooking oil**. Add:
1 lb. of cooked beef, pork, or chicken
Season with salt to taste. Add a bundle of cilantro and cook gently for a few minutes. A good stew to serve with rice.

—Maria Arias
Ontario, CA

Beef Shashlik (kabobs)
Russia

Serves 6

Combine for a marinade:
> ½ c. consommé
> juice of ½ lemon or one small lime
> 8 cloves garlic, minced
> 1 small onion, minced
> 1 T. crushed peppercorns, crushed

Marinate in refrigerator for 8 hours or overnight:
> 3 lbs. boneless lamb or beef sirloin,
> cut in ½" cubes

Allow meat to return to room temperature before cooking. Then toss meat with:
> 3 small onions, cut into wedges
> 3 sweet peppers, seeded and cut into wedges
> 12–15 large mushrooms (optional)
> 12–15 cherry tomatoes or 3 tomatoes,
> cut into wedges

Add a little olive oil or vegetable-oil spray to coat all of the ingredients, patting the meat cubes slightly. Place meat and vegetables on metal skewers, alternating meat and vegetables. Grill or broil skewers, basting with marinade. Salt to taste. Serve with rice.

Sautéed Steak and Potatoes
Argentina

Lomita Saltado
(loh-MEE-tah
sahl-TAH-doh)

Serves 6–8

Cut into 1"x3" strips:
> 3 lbs. sirloin steak, ½" thick

Melt **3 T. butter** in skillet and sauté until browned:
> 3 c. potatoes, peeled and cubed

Heat **4 T. olive oil** in another skillet, then cook steak in it over high heat for 3 minutes, stirring pan frequently. Remove steak and keep warm. In the oil remaining in skillet, sauté for 5 minutes:
> 1½ c. chopped onions

Mix in:
> 1½ c. tomatoes
> 2 t. salt
> ½ t. dried, ground chili peppers

Cook over low heat for 10 minutes. Mix in:
> 2 T. cider vinegar
> 1 c. cooked or canned green beans

Then add the steak and potatoes. Cook over low heat for 10 minutes, mixing occasionally. Taste for seasoning.

Assorted Meat Dinner
Argentina

Puchero Criollo
(pu-CHAIR-oh cree-OH-loh)

This recipe is an Argentinean variation of the Spanish olla podrida *("potful of good things").*

Serves 8–10

Cover with water and bring to boil:

1 c. dried chickpeas

Remove from heat and let soak for 1 hour. Drain. Add **4 qts. of water** and bring to boil again. Add:

2 lbs. short ribs of beef

1 lb. pork, cubed

Cover and cook over medium heat for 1 hour. Then add:

4 lbs. chicken, disjointed

3 Italian sausages, sliced

4 small white onions

2 cloves garlic, minced

Re-cover and cook over low heat for 45 minutes. Add:

4 potatoes, peeled and quartered

8 small carrots

1 lb. yellow squash, peeled and sliced

4 tomatoes, quartered

2-lb. head of cabbage, cut in eighths

1 c. chopped green peppers

6 leeks, cut in half lengthwise

2 t. salt

Re-cover and cook for 45 minutes. Taste for seasoning, then mix in:

3 T. minced parsley

Remove meat and vegetables from the pot and arrange them on a platter. Serve remaining liquid as a soup in deep bowls. Serve both dishes at same time.

Swedish Meatballs
Sweden

Kottbullar
(COAT-beu-lar)

Makes 12–14 small meatballs or 6–8 large meatballs

Sauté in butter until golden brown:
1 T. chopped onions
Soak **7 T. dried white bread crumbs** in the liquid:
1½ t. melted butter
1 c. milk or cream-and-water
Mix together in a bowl:
1 lb. minced beef
¼ lb. minced pork
white pepper to taste
salt to taste
pinch allspice (optional)
Stir in **1 egg** and the fried onions. Add soaked bread crumbs and liquid and beat until smooth. Use small meatballs for a smorgasbord or larger balls served in gravy as a dinner dish.

Small balls: Shape using two teaspoons, dipped in cold water. Heat butter in frying pan and fry a few meatballs at a time for 3–5 minutes. Shake pan so that the balls brown all over and continue to fry over gentle heat, without lid. Serve either hot or cold on smorgasbord.

Large balls: Shape large meatballs the same way, but larger. Fry them for 5–8 minutes. Remove from pan, but keep them hot. Meanwhile swirl out the pan with about **¾ pt. stock** and add about **2 T. thick cream**. The sauce may be thickened more with a little **flour** or **cornstarch** added to the boiling sauce. Season the gravy and serve separately.

Jansson's Temptation
Sweden

Janssons frestelse
(JAN-sons fray-STELL-suh)

Serves 6–8

Peel and slice, then cut slices into thin strips (or use food processor):

6–8 large potatoes

Cover with water. Peel and chop:

2 large onions

Sauté for a few minutes with:

1 large T. butter
⅓ t. pepper
½ t. salt

Heat oven to 375° F. Drain potato strips, then put a layer of strips on bottom of a 9"x13" buttered casserole dish. On top of this, arrange a layer of the chopped onions and:

anchovies (will need a total ½ lb.)

Spread another layer of potato strips, then an anchovy and onion layer, etc. The top layer should be potato strips. Spread over the top layer:

2–3 T. white bread crumbs, crushed

Sprinkle with melted butter. Place in oven for 30 minutes, then add:

½ c. cream

Continue baking for another 15 minutes or until potatoes are well-cooked.

Danish Machine* Cod
Denmark

Maskintorsk
(MASS-kin-TORSK)

Serves 4

*"Machine" refers to the fact that Danes make this recipe using a container with a tightly-fitting lid called "the machine." Our recipe calls for a casserole dish.

Cut into 2" pieces:
1½ lb. cod fillets
Season with **1–2 t. curry powder** and **salt** to taste. Put into a well-greased casserole dish:
2 medium onions, finely chopped
¼ piece celeriac, scraped and grated
Dip the fish in flour and place on top of the vegetables. Spread on top of the cod another:
¼ piece celeriac, scraped and grated
Season with a little salt and put knobs of butter on top. Pour over the fish:
scant ½ cup sparkling grape juice (or water)
½ cup cream
Cover dish with lid or foil. Cook for about 20–30 minutes in a 450° F. oven. Serve with French bread.

Mealtime brings together the extended family at this home in Russia.

Pork Chops and Potatoes
France

Les Cotes de Porc a la Campagnarde
(lay COATS
duh PORK
a la kam-pan-YARD)

Serves 4

Remove and discard rind from:

¼" thick slice salt pork

Cut pork into ¼" matchstick-like slices. Blanch these in boiling water for 5 minutes, drain, and rinse in running water. Pat completely dry with paper towels. Heat a heavy skillet and sauté these pork strips gently until they are golden brown. Remove and set aside. Prepare as follows:

4 ½"-thick pork loin chops

Pat **½ t. pepper** into the chops and dredge them in flour. (Brush off and save the excess flour.) Brown the chops well on both sides in the pork drippings, remove them from frying pan. Then sprinkle them with:

4 juniper berries, crushed

Set the chops aside. Add to the pork drippings in the frying pan:

2 medium-size onions, peeled and quartered
½ t. rubbed sage
1 bay leaf

Sauté them briefly, stirring all the while with a wooden spatula so that the onions come apart and are well-coated with the hot fat. When onions begin to turn translucent, sprinkle the reserve flour over them with a little salt. Stir until flour is absorbed. Add:

2 c. whole milk

Stir until the sauce begins to thicken. Set aside. Preheat oven to 325° F. Put pork strips and chops back into the skillet. Pour sauce over them. Cover pan and put it on the center rack of the oven to bake for 1 hour. Boil in lightly salted water for 15 minutes:

3 large potatoes, peeled and quartered

Drain and put them in with the chops. Bake chops and potatoes uncovered for about 20 minutes or until the potatoes are nicely browned. Serve chops in a heated serving dish with the onion sauce poured over them and the potatoes arranged around the sides of the dish. (*Note*: For added zest, add **1 T. cider vinegar** and **½ t. sugar** to the sauce before pouring over the chops.)

Little Chicken Legs
Brazil

Coxinhas
(cock-ZEE-nahs)

Serves 30

In a 4-qt. Dutch oven, combine:

2½–3 lbs. chicken (broiler or fryer), cut up
3 c. water
1 t. salt

Cover and simmer for 1 hour or until chicken is tender. Drain, reserving 1 cup broth. Remove skin and bones from chicken and discard them. Chop chicken meat and set aside. In a saucepan, melt:

2 T. margarine

Blend in:

¾ c. rice flour
1 t. salt
⅛ t. pepper

Stir in the reserved broth and:

1 c. milk

Cook and stir until the mixture thickens and bubbles. Gradually stir about 1 cup of this hot mixture into:

2 beaten egg yolks

Return this mixture to saucepan. Cook and stir 2 minutes more. Cool, then stir in chopped chicken. Cover and chill.

Using about 2 T. of the chilled chicken mixture, form to shape of chicken leg. Roll in bread crumbs, dip in beaten egg, then roll again in bread crumbs. Insert wooden skewer for handle. Fry a few at a time in hot oil (about 375° F.) until golden brown, about 3 minutes. Drain.

Spinach Cheese Manicotti
Italy

Serves 4

In a small skillet, sauté for 3 minutes:

1 medium onion, finely chopped
3 garlic cloves, minced
1 T. vegetable oil

Set aside. In a mixing bowl, combine:

1½ c. ricotta cheese
½ c. mozzarella cheese
4 oz. cream cheese, softened
4 T. Parmesan cheese
1 t. Italian seasoning
½ t. pepper

Beat ingredients until smooth. Stir in the onion mixture and:

10-oz. pkg. frozen chopped spinach, thawed and squeezed dry

Spoon or pipe into:

8 manicotti shells, cooked and drained

Pour half of a **26-oz. jar spaghetti sauce** into greased 13"x9"x2" baking dish. Arrange the stuffed manicotti shells over the sauce, then top with rest of sauce. Cover and bake at 350° F. for 25 minutes. Uncover; sprinkle with:

½ cup mozzarella cheese
2 T. Parmesan cheese

Bake 5–10 minutes longer or until cheese is melted.

Peasant Pork Stew

Germany

Serves 8

Heat in a heavy skillet:

4 T. vegetable oil

Add:

2 lbs. pork shoulder, cut into 1½" cubes

Brown the cubes on all sides over medium-high heat. Remove pork from skillet and set aside. In another skillet, sauté until they are golden:

3 medium onions, sliced

6 T. butter

Remove and set aside, reserving the butter. Preheat oven to 375° F. In a shallow baking dish, arrange half of:

3 potatoes, peeled and sliced

Cover them with alternating layers of the browned meat, sautéed onions, and:

2 carrots, julienned

1 c. shredded white cabbage

1½ t. caraway seeds

salt and pepper to taste

Make a top layer of potatoes and pour over them the reserved butter drippings. Add:

1 c. beef stock or broth

Put the stew in the oven and bake it, covered, for 1 hour. Uncover stew and bake for another 30 minutes, allowing the top layer of potatoes to brown. Serve in the baking dish.

Lamb Stew
France

Serves 4

Le Navarin
(luh na-vah-RIN)

Wash and dry:

**1½ lbs. breast or neck of lamb, cut into
bite-size pieces**

Sprinkle with:

½ t. pepper

Dredge in:

½ c. flour

Heat in a Dutch oven:

2 T. vegetable oil
3 T. butter

When fat is bubbling, add the meat and brown it. Stir with wooden spatula from time to time so that it doesn't stick. Add:

**3 medium carrots, scraped, trimmed,
cut into ¼" roundels**
3 medium onions, coarsely chopped

Stir them well, coating them with the hot fat. When onions are almost transparent, add:

3 c. water

Drop in a bundle of seasonings in cheesecloth tied securely with cotton thread. The bundle should contain:

1 bay leaf
1 branch celery
1 branch rosemary
1 branch parsley

Cover pot and simmer on low heat for 1 hour. Then add:

6 medium turnips, peeled, quartered
1 t. salt

Simmer for 30–40 minutes, uncovered. Skim off and discard any fat on surface. Discard the bundle of seasonings. Serve very hot.

Mixed Seafood Stew
Argentina

Guisado de Pescado
(gwi-ZAH-doh day pes-CAH-doh)

Serves 6–8

Combine in a saucepan:
> 1½ c. water
> 3 c. bottled clam juice
> ¼ c. grated onion
> 1 T. minced parsley

Bring to boil, then cook over low heat for 10 minutes. Add:
> 1 lb. raw shrimp, shelled, deveined, and
>   quartered
> ½ lb. scallops, quartered
> ½ lb. crab meat
> ½ t. pepper

Cook over low heat for 10 minutes. Mix in:
> 10 oysters, coarsely chopped
> 2 T. butter

Simmer for 3 minutes. Taste for seasoning and serve in deep plates.

Shellfish Savory Rice
Brazil

Arroz de Marisco
(air-ROW day mah-REE-skoh)

Serves 4

Place in a bowl:
> 8 oz. peeled, raw shrimp
> 8 oz. white crab meat

Toss with:
> juice of 1 lime
> 3 sprigs fresh cilantro, chopped
> salt and pepper to taste

In a frying pan, sauté in a little olive oil until soft:
> 1 onion, minced

Stir in:
> 1 large tomato, skinned and seeded
> 1 t. tomato paste

Add the shrimp and crab meat. When very hot, add:
> 20 mussels, scrubbed and bearded
> 4–8 fresh oysters or clams in shell

Cover and cook until all the shells open in the steam, which should take only a few minutes. Add another:
> juice of 1 lime

Check seasoning, then stir in:
> 4 c. boiled long-grain white rice

Heat through until the rice is steaming and has absorbed the flavors of the seafood.

Pasta and Fagioli
Italy

(fah-JOE-lee)

Serves 4

Heat in large skillet or heavy casserole dish:
1 T. olive oil
Sauté over low heat until onions are soft and translucent:
1 medium onion, finely chopped (1½ cups)
3 garlic cloves, pressed
Add:
1 lb. tomatoes, peeled, seeded, diced
1 t. dried oregano, crushed
½ t. dried thyme
½ t. dried rosemary, crushed
½ t. dried marjoram, crushed
⅛ t. red pepper flakes
¼ t. salt
¼ t. pepper
Simmer until sauce is thick and hot, about 10 minutes.
Add:
15-oz. can white kidney or navy beans, rinsed and drained
½ c. water
Cook about 5–8 minutes to heat through. Stir in:
8 oz. spiral pasta, cooked and drained
½ c. finely chopped parsley
½ t. balsamic vinegar
To serve, spoon 1¼ c. mixture onto each of four plates and top with **1 T. freshly grated Parmesan cheese**.

Skinny Pizza
Italy

Serves 4

Let thaw until pliable:
> **1 lb. frozen loaf of bread dough (white or honey wheat)**

Stretch or roll to fit greased 13" round pizza pan or 13"x19" cookie sheet. Spread evenly over dough to within ½" of all edges:
> **6-oz. can pizza sauce**

Sprinkle evenly over pizza:
> **8 oz. grated Monterey Jack cheese**

Arrange over cheese:
> **½ green pepper, cut in rings**
> **1 zucchini, sliced**
> **1 small bunch broccoli (use flowerettes)**
> **5 medium mushrooms, sliced**
> **½ medium onion, cut in strips**

Bake in 425° F. oven for 20 minutes or until crust is golden brown and cheese bubbly.

Vegetable Garden Pizza
Italy

Pizza Giardiniera
(PEET-zah gee-ar-din-EER-ah)

Makes 2 12" pizzas

Preheat oven to 450° F. Top **two 12" Italian bread shells** with:
> **26-oz. jar pasta sauce, either tomato or tomato and basil**
> **2 c. shredded mozzarella cheese**
> **chopped fresh basil or oregano leaves**
> **choice of pizza toppings:**
> > **coarsely chopped or sliced red, green, or yellow peppers**
> > **sliced ripe olives**
> > **chopped or sliced sun-dried tomatoes**
> > **sliced fresh mushrooms**
> > **sliced pepperoni**

Bake 10–12 minutes or until hot and bubbly. Let stand 5 minutes.

Calzone
Italy

Makes 2 calzones, 3–4
servings each

3 oz. each: salami, ham, mortadella
1 T. butter

Let thaw until pliable:

1 lb. loaf frozen bread dough

Sauté in melted butter:

½ medium onion, chopped

Cut meats into ¼" wide strips:

3 oz. salami
3 oz. ham
3 oz. mortadella

Mix meats in a large bowl with the sautéed onions and:

4 oz. mozzarella cheese, grated
8 oz. Ricotta cheese
1 t. oregano
1 T. dried parsley
½ t. thyme
¼ t. salt
¼ t. pepper

Divide bread dough in half. On a lightly floured board, roll each dough piece out to a 10" diameter circle. Place each circle on a lightly greased cookie sheet. Divide meat filling and spread over half of each dough circle. Fold remaining dough over filling and seal by pinching edges lightly. Cut slits on top of each calzone. Bake in 350° F. oven for 30 minutes or until golden brown. Remove from pan and serve immediately.

Berrocks
Russia

Makes 8–10

Mix until loose and fine:
1 lb. ground chuck
1 lb. ground round
1 pkg. Lipton's® onion soup
Heat this mixture in a kettle and and let simmer until tender; drain any fat. In another kettle, put **2 T. cooking oil** and sauté until almost done:
3 large onions
Shred and add to onions:
1 medium head of cabbage
Cook uncovered until cabbage is translucent. (Don't overcook!) Drain any moisture. Mix cabbage and meat mixture well; season with salt and pepper. Let stand until dough is ready.

Dough:
Any bread mix or frozen dough will work with the recipe. Begin by rolling out the bread dough to ⅛–⅜" thickness. Cut dough into 5" circles and place a rounded tablespoon of the berrock mixture in the center of dough. Fold over to form crescent and pinch edges together to enclose and seal. Place on greased baking sheet, pinched sides down and not too close together. Bake at 375° F. about 30–35 minutes, until they're as brown as you like.

—*Katherine Manske*

Uralski Pelmeni
Russia

Serves 4–6

Sift together:

3 cups flour
½ t. salt

Make a well in the middle and put **1 egg** and **½ c. water** in it. Knead until dough is pliable. Roll out thinly. Cut into circles about 2½" inches in diameter. Sauté in a skillet:

½ lb. beef
½ lb. pork
1 onion, chopped

Place a small portion of the sautéed filling ingredients on half the dough circle. Fold over and seal. Simmer in a large kettle of boiling water until pastry is cooked. Drain and serve with butter or sour cream.

—*Mary Faducovich Hart*

Building Diversity

Relationships with people of other cultures should be based on genuine friendship and respect, not just on spiritual and social issues. Get to know others who are in a different economic position, whether more affluent or more needy than you. Forums for meeting others might include:

- eating in ethnic restaurants or learning to cook ethnic foods;

- joining in a service project with a culturally different church;

- taking a prayer walk through your community and greeting those you pass along the way;

- teaming up with a Christian brother or sister of a different race to study the Bible together;

- moving into a neighborhood/community where cultural diversity exists.

—*Matthew Bye*
Cincinnati, OH

Desserts

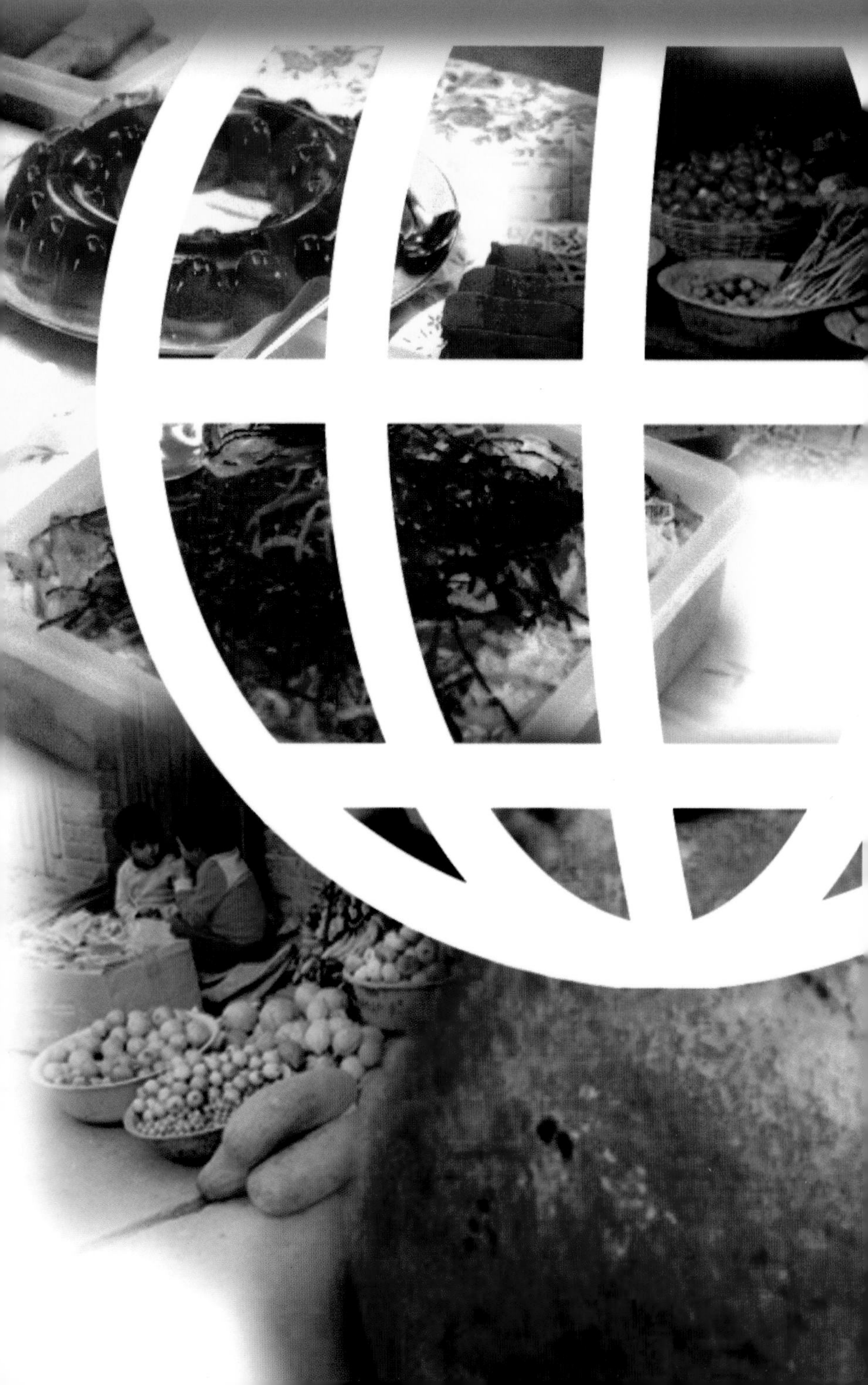

Hospitality in Scandinavia

Per (Peter) Johansson grew up in the small town of Skane, in southern Sweden. "The midsummer celebration sticks in my mind," he says. "I remember the little girls with the flower wreaths in their hair, the maypole, and the food. We had herring a dozen different ways, sour dough bread, potatoes of every kind, and those early strawberries. I loved it."

Early Vikings had a very limited supply of food and preserved it by salting, smoking, and drying, and these methods are still popular among Scandinavian peoples. Or as one common saying goes, "the Finns cure lamb in their saunas." Seafood is clearly the largest source of protein for the countries of north Europe. Restaurants feature *dagensrath* (or "fish of the day"), and this can mean anything from arctic cod to trout, pike, salmon, mackerel, or the overwhelming favorite, herring. Shrimp, oysters, eels, mussels, and crayfish are regular favorites.

Even Americans are familiar with the word, *Smorgasbord*. This Swedish term literally means "the whole bread-and-butter table." The start of this meal is a sandwich of herring on dark, multi-grain black bread. This is placed on a *smorrebraet* (buttering board) and various foods are added to it to make an open-faced sandwich (*smorrebord*). Everything on the traditionally bountiful spread is then available to be added to the sandwich. These items are called *paalaeg* (the "laid-on things").

St. Lucia's Day (*Luciadagen*) in December—the shortest day of the year—probably got its name from the root of the word, *lux*, Latin for *light*. On this day in Sweden a very special series of celebrations take place, all revolving around the consumption of Scandinavian pastry. The eldest daughter arises early, dresses in a white gown and wire crown to represent the *Lussibruden* ("Lucia's bride"). The crown is elaborate, including seven or nine lighted candles and a wreath of fir and lingonberry twigs. She wakes the rest of the family with songs, coffee, and round twisted saffron buns with raisin eyes in them called *lussekattort* ("Lucia cats").

The family soon gathers for a huge breakfast, a portion of which is held back to share with animals of the household. A special three-legged bowl holds a sweet drink that is traditionally served on this holiday. All during the day, the family joins in baking special cookies and cakes, preparing for the season just ahead.

In Denmark, Christmas Eve (*Juleaften*) is celebrated first by attending a church service, followed by a festive meal of roast goose, stuffed with apples and prunes and served with red cabbage. An important part of the dinner is the *risengrod*, a rice pudding cooked with cinnamon and butter and an almond. Whoever finds the almond in his portion receives a prize.

Rice Pudding
India

Kheer
(KHEER)

Serves 4

Boil until soft in **1½ cups water:**
1 c. white rice
Add and stir well while simmering (about 30 minutes):
1 can sweetened condensed milk diluted with 2
cansful of water
½ c. raisins
pistachio nuts
1 t. anise seed
Keep mixture moist by adding milk or water. When creamy in texture, place in bowl and garnish with slivered almonds. Serve either cold or warm.

—Allen and Leoda Buckwalter
Elizabethtown, PA (India)

Christmas Rice Pudding
Sweden

Serves 4-6

The custom in Sweden is to mix one bleached almond into the Christmas pudding. If a single girl gets the almond, it forecasts that she will marry within a year.

Bring to a boil, being careful not to scorch:
1 qt. milk
Add:
1 c. rice
Simmer until rice is tender. Beat in:
4 eggs
¾ c. sugar
1 t. vanilla
Mix well and pour into casserole dish; sprinkle **cinnamon** on top. Bake at 350° F. approximately 30–40 minutes or until set.

French Rice Pudding
France

Le Riz au Lait
(luh-REES ou-LAY)

Serves 4–5

Outside of France, cinnamon is a common garnish to rice pudding, but don't tell your French friends. They would be shocked.

Bring **3 c. water** to a rolling boil. Add:

½ c. rice, picked over and well washed

Cook for 5 minutes and place in a fine colander. Rinse in cold water and set aside to drain. Slowly heat milk with lemon peel and vanilla in heavy pot:

3 c. whole milk

peel of 1 lemon, carefully removed in one continuous spiral

1 t. vanilla extract

Simmer 5 minutes, then remove and discard lemon peel. Add rice to this mixture, along with:

¼ c. granulated sugar

½ t. salt

Simmer at the lowest heat for half an hour, stirring occasionally to prevent rice from scorching at the bottom. Swirl in:

2 T. sweet butter

Remove pot from heat. Put pudding into serving bowl. Can be served hot or cold.

Baked Rice Pudding
England

Serves 4–6

Put the following ingredients in a lightly greased baking dish and stir to mix:

½ c. rice

¼ c. brown sugar, packed

4 c. milk

Dot with **1 oz. butter** cut into small pieces and place in preheated oven at 300° F. Bake for 2½ hours or until the liquid is absorbed and the rice is tender. Stir once or twice during the cooking period.

—Judy Smith and June Simmonds
London, England

Flan or Custard
Venezuela

Quesillo
(kay-SEE-yoh)

Serves 12

Desserts are not commonly eaten with dinner in Venezuela.

To carmelize sugar, brown in casserole or baking pan with lid:

¼ c. white sugar

Let it brown well, tipping from side to side to coat bottom of pan. Beat thoroughly in a bowl:

5 eggs

Add to beaten eggs:

1 can sweetened condensed milk
1 can fresh milk (use sweetened condensed milk can to measure)
½ t. vanilla

Pour this mixture into caramelized sugar, cover, and place in a pan of boiling water on top of the stove. Boil for about ½ hour or until the *quesillo* is set. To test, remove the lid and insert a knife. If the knife comes out clean, the *quesillo* is done. Remove from hot water. When cool, invert on a platter. The carmelized sugar, which liquefies in the process, keeps the *quesillo* from sticking to the pan. Refrigerate and serve cold.

—*Thata Book*
Manheim, PA (Venezuela)

Persimmon Custard
Japan

Combine and pour into greased baking dish:

2 c. persimmon pulp, scooped from persimmon
½ c. sugar
2 egg yolks, slightly beaten
½ t. soda
¼ t. cinnamon
⅛ t. nutmeg
pinch of salt

Set baking dish in pan of hot water and bake slowly, about 325° F. for 15 minutes. To make meringue, beat until stiff:

2 egg whites
¼ c. sugar
pinch of salt

Place meringue on top of custard and bake until slightly browned.

—*Lucille Graybill*
Osaka, Japan

Pumpkin Custard Pie and Cups
United States / Pennsylvania Dutch

Serves 12

Separate 3 eggs. Beat whites until stiff and set aside. Beat yolks and add:

2 c. mashed pumpkin (or canned)
2 c. sugar
¼ c. margarine or butter, melted
½ c. flour

Stir in:

1 qt. milk, powdered or skim

Fold in beaten egg whites. Pour into 9" pastry-lined pie pan and 6 custard cups. Sprinkle with cinnamon. Place custard cups in a pan and add 1" of hot water. Bake pie and custard cups at 400° F. for 10 minutes. Reduce temperature to 350° F. and bake 45 minutes longer.

—Mrs. Herbert Kreider
Hershey, PA

Granadilla Pudding
Zimbabwe

Serves 6

Heat in double boiler:

2½ c. milk

Mix together in a bowl:

1 egg, beaten
¼ c. sugar
3 T. cornstarch
¼ t. salt
½ c. milk

Gradually stir the mixture into the hot milk. Cook and stir until thickened. Blend in:

1 T. margarine
1¼ t. vanilla

Chill slightly, then add:

4 granadilla or passion fruit, pulp only

Mix well and serve cold.

—Mildred Yoder
Bulawayo, Zimbabwe

Amaretto Chocolate Mousse
Italy

Serves 4

In saucepan, combine:

⅓ cup sugar
2 tablespoons flour
2 tablespoons unsweetened cocoa
¾ cup milk

Cook and stir until thickened; cook and stir 2 minutes longer. Stir hot mixture into **2 egg yolks**, then return to saucepan. Cook and stir until bubbly, then cook and stir 2 minutes longer. Remove from heat. Stir in:

1 T. butter or margarine
1 T. amaretto

Cover surface with plastic wrap; chill 1–2 hours or until cooled but not set. Whip until soft peaks form:

¾ c. whipping cream

Fold about ¼ of the whipping cream into chocolate mixture, then fold in remaining cream. Cover and chill. Refrigerate leftovers.

Wet-Bottom Shoo Fly Pie
United States/ Pennsylvania Dutch

Serves 6–8

Mix together:

1 c. flour
⅔ c. brown sugar
1 T. shortening

Set aside ½ c. of these crumbs for topping. To the remaining crumbs, add the following mixture:

1 t. baking soda dissolved in ¾ c. hot water
1 c. molasses
1 egg, well beaten
1 t. vanilla

Pour into unbaked pie shell and sprinkle the remaining ½ c. crumbs on top of pie. Bake for 10 minutes at 425° F., then at 350° F. until brown (20–25 minutes).

—*Lois Jean Peterman*
Lancaster, PA

Plum Pudding
United States / Navajo

Serves 4–6

I found this recipe in one of the kitchen cupboards at the Navajo Mission. It was an ingenious way to use plums, of which we had a generous supply.

Combine all ingredients in a saucepan:

16-oz. can plums or 1 lb. fresh plums
¾ T. tapioca
⅓ t. almond extract
½ c. sugar (less if using canned plums)
dash of salt
several drops red food coloring

Bring to boil and simmer until slightly thickened. This can be served as a pudding or as a pie filling.

—*Marilyn Smith*
Souderton, PA
(Navajo Mission, NM)

Rich Egg Custard
England

Serves 4

Mix the following ingredients thoroughly in a 1-qt. baking dish:

4 eggs
3 T. sugar
2 c. milk

Sprinkle ½ **t. grated nutmeg** over the mixture. Put baking dish into a deep baking tin half-filled with cold water. Bake in oven preheated to 325° F. for 45 minutes or until set.

—*Judy Smith and June Simmonds*
London, England

Cassava Cake
Malawi

Serves 8

Cassava *is a root that may be purchased in season in the fresh-fruit section of many supermarkets.*

Beat well:
    2 eggs
Add:
    ¾ c. sugar
    3 T. melted shortening or butter
    ¾ c. coconut milk
Add and mix well:
    1 c. fresh cassava, grated
    ½ c. young coconut (optional)
Fold in:
    4 T. grated cheese
Pour into greased 9"x9" pan. Bake at 350° F. for 40 minutes. Brush with **1 T. butter**, then sprinkle top with a little sugar and bake for an additional 5 minutes or until golden brown.

—Mel Andricks
Mangochi, Malawi

Carrot Pudding
India

Gajar Halva
(GAH-jer HAL-vah)

Serves 8

In a heavy saucepan, heat:
    4 c. whole milk
Add:
    1 lb. carrots, finely grated
Bring to boil and continue boiling slowly for 2–3 hours.
Add:
    1 can sweetened condensed milk
    ½ c. sugar
Continue cooking over low heat for another ½ hour, stirring occasionally. Then add:
    ½ c. butter
Cook for another 10 minutes. Remove from heat and stir in:
    8 whole cardamoms
Garnish with **¼ c. sliced almonds** and **raisins**. Serve hot (may be slightly runny).

—Mary Roy
Bihar, India

Deluxe English Trifle
England

Serves 9–12

Bake in 2 round layers and cool:
one yellow cake mix
Cook (or use instant) and cool:
1 6-oz. package vanilla pudding mix, using ½ c. extra milk
Split one layer of cake in two. Put top half on a plate. Put other half in bottom of flat-bottom glass bowl (trimmed to size of bowl). Drain:
20-oz. can fruit cocktail (reserve juice)
Pour the juice over the two split layers of cake. Pour ½ of the fruit over the cake in the glass bowl. Pour ½ of the pudding over the fruit. Repeat the three layers: cake, fruit, and pudding. Cover and refrigerate several hours. Before serving, spread top with sweetened whipped cream or Cool Whip®. Decorate with cherries or slivered almonds. To serve, spoon into dessert dishes.

—*Leone Sider*
Grantham, PA

Cake without Baking
Argentina

Torta Sin Hornear

(TORE-tas in hoar-NEAR)

Serves 16

Open:
pkg. of 48 rectangular chocolate cookies
Dip 16 cookies in:
1 c. milk
Lay out in single layer in a shallow cake pan, forming a square. Mix together until smooth and spreadable:
1 c. melted caramel (*Dulce de Leche* can be used; see recipe.)
1 c. cream cheese
Spread caramel mixture over cookie base. Repeat more layers till you're out of cookies. Put in refrigerator for 1 hour before serving.

An Arab tour guide poses for the camera near the pyramids, Eygpt. Photo © Corbis.

Mexican Fruit Cake
United States / Southern

Beat together:
> **1½ c. sugar**
> **2 eggs**

Mix together and add to egg mixture:
> **2 c. flour**
> **2 t. baking soda**

Stir in:
> **20-oz. can crushed pineapple with juice**
> **1 c. chopped nuts**

Bake in ungreased 9"x13" pan at 350° F. for 35 minutes. Use electric mixer to mix icing:
> **8 oz. cream cheese (low fat or regular)**
> **1 t. vanilla**
> **½ stick margarine**

Add:
> **2 c. powdered sugar**

Spread on cake while still warm. Chill before serving. This freezes well and can be served right from the freezer.

> —*Vanessa Rubley*
> *McMinnville, TN*

213

Chocolate Butter Cream Torte
Germany

Serves 6–8

Step 1:
Beat until foamy:
6 egg whites, room temperature
Gradually add:
⅓ c. sugar
Beat until stiff peaks form. Beat together:
6 egg yolks
½ c. sugar
When thick and pale yellow, fold into whites. Gradually fold in:
1 c. flour
Evenly divide the batter into 6 greased and floured 9" cake pans. Bake at 350 F. for 10–12 minutes.

Step 2:
Mix well in the top of a double boiler:
¾ cup sugar
3 whole eggs
2 egg yolks
2-oz. semi-sweet chocolate chips
1 t. instant coffee
1 t. pure vanilla
Cook, stirring over simmering water for 10–15 minutes or until thick. Cool completely. With electric mixer, beat until fluffy:
1 c. unsalted butter, softened
Gradually mix into chocolate mixture. Alternate the cake layers with 2 cans **cherry pie filling** and **butter cream.**

—*Hyla Klabunde*

Indian Pudding
Canada / Cree

Serves 12–16

This would be made for winter holidays. The Cree didn't have ovens on the trapline and so, by boiling, this dessert was made possible.

Measure into a large bowl:

4 c. flour

Cut in:

¼ c. margarine

Add the following ingredients:

2 T. baking powder
¼ t. salt
¼ t. allspice
¼ t. cinnamon
¼ c. currants
½ c. raisins

Mix the following ingredients in a separate bowl and add to above:

½ c. brown sugar
1½ c. molasses
½ c. white sugar
¼ t. salt
½ c. water

Lightly grease 4 12-oz. coffee tins. Cut circles of wax paper and place in bottoms of tins. Divide dough into the 4 tins. Cover tins with aluminum foil. Put large kettle (canner) on stove with rack in bottom, and add 2" of water. Put puddings in kettle on rack, cover and steam 3 hours. Add more boiling water if necessary. Lift from kettle, remove foil, and cool for 20 minutes. Run a table knife around pudding, gently shake loose, and remove from tins. Cool right side up until cold. Cover with cloth while cooling. To serve, reheat pudding in oven or microwave or return to a coffee tin, cover, and steam about 45 minutes. Serve with milk (optional).

—*Jennie Rensberry*
LaLoche, SK
Leone Sider
Grantham, PA

Banana Tart
Brazil

Torta de Banana
(TORE-tah day
ba-NAN-nah)

Serves 6–8

Peel **4 large bananas** and press through sieve. Mix the banana pulp in a saucepan with:

½ c. sugar
⅛ t. salt
1 T. butter

Stir and cook until mixture starts to boil, then remove from heat and allow to cool. (*Note*: If firmer mixture is desired, add 1 t. softened plain gelatin at this point.) When cool, whip in:

juice of 1 lime
½ t. nutmeg

Pour into baked pie shell. Top with whipped cream.

Rosy Rhubarb
United States / Pennsylvania Dutch

Serves 10-12

Sift together:

2 c. flour
¼ t. salt
2½ t. baking powder

Then cut **½ c. margarine** into the flour mix. Add and work into a dough:

1 egg, slightly beaten
¾ c. milk

Spread into greased 9"x13" pan, bringing up around sides a bit. Spread onto the dough:

6 c. diced rhubarb

Sprinkle over the rhubarb:

3 oz. red Jell-O® (powder)

To make a topping, crumble the following ingredients with fingers and spread on top:

6 T. margarine
1¼ c. sugar
½ c. flour

Then sprinkle with another **1 oz. red Jell-O® (powder)**. Bake at 350° F. for 30–40 minutes. May serve with milk or ice cream, but it is delicious served plain.

—*Millie Sollenberger*
Hagerstown, MD

Wild Cranberry Bars
Canada / Cree

Combine in a 2-qt. saucepan:
- **2 c. wild (fresh or frozen) cranberries**
- **¼ c. water**
- **1 c. sugar**

Bring to a boil, stirring to prevent sticking. Reduce heat and simmer 10 minutes. Mash berries. Combine in a bowl:
- **1½ c. quick cooking rolled oats**
- **1 c. flour**
- **¼ t. baking soda**
- **½ c. brown sugar**
- **¼ t. salt**

Cut into the above ingredients:
- **½ c. butter**

Press half of this crust mixture into an 8"x8" pan. Spread cranberry sauce over the crust, and sprinkle with remaining crumbs.

Variation:
Substitute a 15½-oz. can of cranberry sauce for the fresh or frozen cranberries.

—*Koonu Goulet*
Saskatchewan, Canada

Persimmon Bars
Japan

Persimmons are plentiful in Japan, so Christian missionaries found many ways to use the overabundance of soft fruit.

Mix all ingredients well to create a thick batter:

1 c. soft persimmon pulp
1 c. sugar
1 c. flour
½ c. milk
½ t. cinnamon
½ t. nutmeg
2 t. baking soda
1 T. butter
pinch salt

Pour batter into 8"x9" pan. Bake at 250° F. for 45 minutes.

—*Ruth Zook*
Mechanicsburg, PA (Japan)

Peanut Crunches
Zimbabwe

Makes 2 dozen cookies

Missionaries often use this recipe when they return from village visitation with gifts of peanuts or "monkey nuts" they have received in appreciation for their visits.

Beat until thick and lemon-colored:

1 egg
Add and mix well:
¼ c. sugar
⅛ t. salt
Add and stir:
2 c. raw peanuts, chopped

Drop by small spoonsful on a greased cookie sheet; mash cookies flat. Bake at 350° F. for 15 minutes until edges begin to brown.

—*Grace Holland*
Ashland, OH (Zimbabwe)

Lemon Squares
Québec

Miettes au citron
(ME-et oh SEH-trohn)

Serves 12

Mix together and heat in saucepan over medium heat until thickened, bubbling slightly:
   2 c. sugar
   2 c. water
   4 T. cornstarch
Remove from heat and add:
   2 eggs, slightly beaten
Return to heat for 2–3 minutes. Stir constantly. Remove from heat and cool to room temperature. Then add:
   ⅓ c. lemon juice (adjust to taste)
Mix the following crumb mixture in a bowl:
   1¾ c. of plain soda crackers (unsalted), crumbled
   ¾ c. flour
   ¾ c. sugar
   1 t. baking powder
   ¾ c. butter (cut in with knife)
   ¾ c. coconut
Place half of crumb mixture in an 8"x8" pan. Spread with filling, cooled to room temperature. Cover with rest of crumb mixture. Bake at 375° F. about 30 minutes or until coconut is golden brown.

—*Thérèse Baillargeon*
St. Romuald, Québec

Centennial Cookies
Russia

Stolentneye pechenye
(sto-LENT-nee PEH-che-NEE)

Makes approx. 24 cookies

Beat together until creamy and pale yellow:
   ½ c. butter, cut up in pieces
   1¾ c. sugar
Gradually stir in:
   6 eggs
Mix in:
   2 c. potato flour
   grated peel of 1 lemon
Drop walnut-size cookies, 1" apart, on a greased baking sheet. Bake in a 375 F. oven until golden brown, approx. 20 minutes.

Persimmon Cookies
Japan

Cream together until fluffy:
  ½ c. softened butter or margarine
  1 c. granulated sugar
Add to above mixture and beat well:
  1 large egg
Then add and mix well:
  1 c. strained persimmon pulp
  1 t. soda
  1 t. vanilla
Sift together in a separate bowl:
  1 c. all-purpose flour
  1 t. cinnamon
  1 t. nutmeg
  ½ t. salt
Add the following:
  1 c. raisins, chopped
  1 c. nuts, chopped
Combine persimmon and nut mixtures and mix well. Drop by teaspoonsful onto greased baking sheets and bake at 350° F. for 12 minutes.

—Lucille Graybill
Osaka, Japan

Russian Tea Cakes
Russia

Makes about 48 cookies

Cream together:
  1 c. butter
  ½ c. sifted 10x sugar
  1 t. vanilla
Add:
  2¼ c. sifted flour
  ¼ t. salt
  ¾ c. chopped nuts (usually pecans)
Chill the dough 1 hour, then roll into 1" balls. Place on ungreased cookie sheet about 2½" apart. Bake until set but not brown in a 375° F. oven, about 10–12 minutes. While still warm, roll in powdered sugar. Allow to cool. Before storing, roll again in powdered sugar.

—Barbara Harman

We need to remember that the normal meal for many people around the world is rice, beans, or bread served with one other item, probably a simply prepared vegetable. The following menus could be used for special guest meals or church fellowship meals.

Africa

Peanut Soup (Zambia) 32
Spinach and Rice Pondo (Zaire) 175
Rice and Raisin Salad (South Africa) 60
Cassava Cake (Malawi) 211

Argentina

Baked Tomatoes 97
Squash and Corn 93
Sautéed Steak and Potatoes 187
Cake without Baking 212
Herbal Tea 12

Brazil

Chayote Salad with Oranges 54
Collard Greens 83
Little Chicken Legs 193
Potato Dumplings 178
Banana Tart 216

Canada

Rice Salad 61
English Scones 17
Multi-Meat Pie 148
Wild Cranberry Bars 217
Tea or coffee

England

Egg and Lemon Soup 31
Toad-in-the-Hole 138
Steamed vegetables of choice
Deluxe English Trifle 212
Tea or coffee

France

Menu 1 (Cuisine Bougoisie)
Basic French Green Salad 56
Country Bread 28
Fried Zucchini Slices 84
Grilled Steak 109

Menu 2 (Haute Cuisine)
Potato and Leek Soup 42
Eggs in a Nest 164
Gratin of Boiled Beef with Onion Sauce 111
Eggplant from a French Aunt 91
French Rice Pudding 206

Germany

Macaroni Salad with Hot Dressing 63
Wheat (White) Bread 24
Sweet and Sour Red Cabbage 77
Sauerbraten 115
Chocolate Butter Cream Torte 214

India

Menu 1
Vegetable Fritters 50
Steamed rice
Cabbage and Pea Curry 80
Beef Curry 107
Fresh Tomato Chutney 66
Rice Pudding 205

Menu 2
Cauliflower and Potato Curry 80
Chicken Curry 125
Vegetable Pulau 74
Yogurt
Fresh fruit

Italy

Wedding Soup 44
White Bean Salad 62
Hearty Eggplant Parmesan 181
Spinach Cheese Manicotti 194
Amaretto Chocolate Mousse 209

Japan

Menu 1
Pan Sautéed Meat and Vegetables 116
Pumpkin Cabbage Salad 58
Fresh fruit (e.g., Mandarin oranges)
Green tea

Menu 2
Chicken and Vegetables Cooked in Broth 130
Scrambled Tofu on Rice 186
Persimmon Bars 218
Green tea

Middle East

Hummus (Jordan) 160
Meat and Macaroni (Egypt) 121
Taubolleh (Jordan) 66
Seasonal fruit
Tea

Russia

Beet Salad 59
Black Bread 20
Borscht 38
Beef Stroganov 110
Centennial Cookies 219

Scandinavia

Cucumber Salad (Norway) 59
Caraway and Fennel Seed Bread 27
Glazed Onions (Norway) 98
Stuffed Pork Roast (Denmark) 141
Christmas Rice Pudding (Sweden) 205

United States

Menu 1 (Native American)
Tossed greens
Fry Bread 21
Refried Beans 157
Mutton Stew 136
Plum Pudding 210

Menu 2 (Pennsylvania Dutch)
Sweet Red Beets and Eggs 92
Cabbage Slaw for Freezer 57
German Hot Potato Salad 167
Roast Pig Stomach 138
Wet-Bottom Shoo Fly Pie 209
Rolls
Coffee

RECIPE INDEX

GEOGRAPHICAL INDEX

T

Thailand
Chicken in Coconut Milk 129
Fried Noodles Thai Style 166
Lemon Grass Soup 34
Rice with Red Pork 175
Shrimp and Ground Pork Toast 152

U

United States / Hispanic
Mole de Plátano 75
Pepian 186

United States / Navajo
Chicken Enchilada 131
Chili Beans 155
Enchiladas 151
Fry Bread 21
Kneeldown Bread 20
Liver Sausage 136
Mutton Stew 136
Plum Pudding 210
Refried Beans 157
Spanish Rice 173

United States / Pennsylvania Dutch
Cabbage Relish 58
Cabbage Slaw for Freezer 57
Cooked Dried Corn 85
Corn Pie 88
Fastnachts 15
German Hot Potato Salad 167
Ham Loaf 142
Pumpkin Custard Pie and Cups 208
Roast Pig Stomach 138
Rosy Rhubarb 216
Sauerkraut 77
Sweet Red Beets and Eggs 92
Wet-Bottom Shoo Fly Pie 209

United States / Southern
Cornbread Dressing 30
Cornbread Taco Bake 123
Mexican Fruit Cake 213
Shoe Peg Corn Casserole 89
Squash Dressing 93
Squash Puppies 92

V

Venezuela
Black Beans 155
Festive Ham Bread 22
Flan or Custard 207
Fried Plantains 95
Fruit Drink 11
Pumpkin Soup 33

Z

Zaire
Spinach and Rice Pondo 175

Zambia
Cabbage-Peanut Relish 76
Cornmeal Porridge 169
Curried Meat 122
Fresh Greens with Peanut Butter 79
Peanut Soup 32
Relish 143
Roasted Peanuts 46
Tonga Chicken 130

Zimbabwe
Cabbage with Peanut Butter 75
Cornmeal Porridge 170
Fresh Corn Bread 23
Granadilla Pudding 208
Hominy and Chick Peas 160
Hominy in Peanut Butter Sauce 73
Mixed Grain Dish 170
Mushrooms with Peanut Butter 71
Peanut Crunches 218